MEDICINAL PLANTS OF THE WORLD

Sébastien Mallet

MEDICINAL PLANTS OF THE WORLD

The 35 plants and spices that heal, virtues and preparation of plants to improve health

Disclaimer of liability

Dear Readers, the information presented in this book is intended for educational and informational purposes only. Every effort has been made to ensure the accuracy of this information, its reliability and its verified sources.

The information herein is not intended to be a substitute for professional advice, and the author declines all responsibility for any misinterpretation of this information.

Contents

INTRODUCTION

Welcome, dear readers, to the enchanting world of medicinal plants, these jewels of nature, brimming with mystery and unexplored benefits. I'm Sébastien Mallet, a passionate herbalist who has dedicated many years to studying and understanding the hidden treasures of the plant kingdom. Since my earliest childhood, medicinal plants have been my faithful companions, introducing me to the secrets of nature and the richness of our nourishing earth.

Medicinal plants are extraordinary living beings that embody the very essence of life, healing and nutrition. They reflect ancestral wisdom, a knowledge passed down through the ages, revealing the profound mysteries of life and health. They are silent healers, offering their natural remedies to heal ailments and enrich our lives.

As an herbalist, every day spent with plants is a fascinating journey, an ongoing discovery of their healing properties, delicate aromas and unique flavors. My love for these plants has led me to deepen my knowledge, explore their essence, and share their benefits with the world. I'm delighted to share with you the wonders of the plants that have given me so much.

In this book, I invite you on a journey through the plant kingdom. You'll be introduced to the benefits of medicinal spices, traditional Chinese herbs and other renowned medicinal plants. I'll guide you step by step, revealing the origins, therapeutic properties and culinary applications of each plant. You'll learn how to incorporate these plants into your daily routine to enrich your meals and enhance your well-being.

The aim of this book is to unveil the mystical world of medicinal plants, and to share with you the knowledge and experience I've accumulated over the years. I want you to discover how these wonders of nature can contribute to your health and well-being. This book is not just a guide; it's a companion, a source of inspiration for all those who wish to explore botanical wisdom and rediscover the precious bond that unites us with nature.

Every page is an invitation to discovery and wonder. As you peruse this book, you'll immerse yourself in the fascinating world of plants, and feel my passion and deep respect for these silent healers. I sincerely hope that this book will be a source of knowledge and inspiration for you, and that you will find as much joy and satisfaction in exploring the plant world as I have myself.

I wish you an enriching read and a wonderful journey into the world of medicinal plants. May you, dear readers, discover and embrace the art and science of herbal medicine, and rediscover the intimate, ancestral dialogue between man and plant.

Your opinion counts!

Once you've finished this book, share your review on Amazon.

Your feedback will be useful for future readers.

I look forward to seeing how this book has impacted you.

Thank you in advance for your contribution, and happy reading!

PART I: MEDICINAL SPICES

These medicinal spices are generally commercially available. However, it is advisable to opt for organic products or to buy from specialized stores to guarantee their quality and purity.

GINGER
(Zingiber officinale)

AN ALLY IN YOUR WELL-BEING

Ginger, native to Asia, has been renowned for thousands of years for its medicinal and culinary virtues, a spice that combines gustatory pleasure with exceptional therapeutic benefits.

Ginger, a rhizome with a tangy, lemony taste, is a thousand-year-old spice whose use dates back more than 5,000 years. Native to Asia, it was one of the first spices to be traded on ancient trade routes between Asia and Europe, thanks to its exceptional preservative capacity. Ginger was appreciated by the Greeks and Romans, who used it both in cooking and medicine for its anti-inflammatory and digestive properties. In traditional Chinese medicine, it is reputed to balance yin and yang energies and to treat numerous ailments such as nausea and rheumatism. Ginger is also a key ingredient in Indian Ayurvedic medicine, used to stimulate digestion and the immune system. Finally, in the Middle Ages, ginger found a place of choice in European kitchens, before falling somewhat into disuse, before regaining its letters of nobility in our contemporary kitchens, as much for its exotic flavors as for its many health-promoting properties.

In the kitchen

Ginger is a **versatile**, **aromatic** spice that can enhance many dishes, from starters to desserts. It goes perfectly with chicken, fish, seafood and even fruit. Its tangy, lemony flavor enhances sweet and savory dishes, and its spicy aroma adds depth and warmth to preparations. As well as being a delicious and versatile ingredient, ginger is also **rich in antioxidants**, **anti-inflammatory**, **digestive** and can **boost the immune system**. Regular use can help **improve digestion**, **reduce inflammation**, **fight infection** and **boost the** body's **natural defenses.** In addition, its essential oil is used for its anti-nausea properties and can be beneficial in cases of motion sickness. Finally, its powder is often used in baking to make cookies, cakes and other sweet treats. Whether fresh, powdered, candied or in essential oil form, ginger is a treasure trove of benefits and flavors.

HEALING WITH GINGER

- For **nausea or vomiting,** mix a teaspoon of grated ginger with hot water. Steep for 5 minutes, strain and drink 2-3 times a day.

- For **muscle and joint pain**, apply a paste of fresh ginger to the painful area, leave for 15 minutes, then rinse.

- If you have **digestive problems,** eat a teaspoon of grated ginger mixed with honey before meals.

- To **combat colds and flu,** inhale steam from boiling water mixed with a few slices of ginger for 5-10 minutes, twice a day.

- For **sore throats,** gargle with a ginger decoction 3 times a day.

- For **fatigue,** drink a teaspoon of ginger juice mixed with honey once a day.

- For **menstrual disorders,** apply a warm compress of ginger decoction to the lower abdomen to relieve pain.

GINGER IN THE KITCHEN

Carrot and ginger soup

INGREDIENTS: 500 g carrots, 1 onion, 1 clove garlic, 1 piece fresh ginger (approx. 5 cm), 1 l vegetable stock, 2 tbsp olive oil, salt and pepper.

1. Peel and chop the onion, garlic and ginger.

2. Peel and slice the carrots.

3.   In a saucepan, sauté onion, garlic and ginger in olive oil until tender.

4.   Add the carrots and sauté for a few minutes.

5.   Pour in the vegetable stock, bring to the boil, then lower the heat and simmer until the carrots are tender.

6.   Blend the soup until smooth.

7.   Season with salt and pepper and serve hot. Enjoy!

CURCUMA

(Curcuma longa)

A RAY OF SUNSHINE ON YOUR PLATE

Turmeric, known as "turmeric", is a precious spice renowned for its many health benefits and unique earthy, peppery taste.

Turmeric is a golden spice native to the Indian subcontinent. Used for millennia in traditional Indian and Asian cooking and medicine, it is a key ingredient in the spice blend known as curry. It is a powerful anti-inflammatory and antioxidant, and is said to have anti-cancer properties. This spice has played a central role in Ayurveda, the traditional Indian medicine, to treat various ailments such as inflammations, infections, digestive disorders and skin diseases. Turmeric was introduced to Europe in the Middle Ages by Arab traders. It was used as a medicine, but also as a textile dye due to its intense yellow color. Today, turmeric continues to be an essential element in cuisines the world over, and is increasingly recognized for its health benefits, thanks to the bioactive compound curcumin, which gives it its medicinal properties and characteristic color.

In the kitchen

Turmeric is a **versatile, aromatic** spice that can add a touch of color and flavor to a wide variety of dishes. It goes particularly well with vegetable, rice, meat and fish dishes, adding a sweet, earthy nuance to preparations. **Antioxidant, anti-inflammatory** and rich in **curcumin,** turmeric is not only tasty, but also beneficial to health. It is reputed to **improve digestion, support the immune system**, and may play a role in **preventing chronic diseases** such as cancer and heart disease. As a drink, turmeric-based golden milk is a traditional Indian beverage, tasty and comforting, which highlights the healing properties of this spice. In powder form, it's easy to incorporate into sauces, stews and soups for a boost of flavor and color. Used in moderation, turmeric can be a delicious and healthy ally to enrich your daily diet and bring an exotic note to your meals.

HEALING WITH TURMERIC

- To **reduce inflammation**, mix a teaspoon of turmeric powder in a glass of warm milk and drink this mixture once a day.

- For a **sore throat,** gargle with warm water mixed with a teaspoon of turmeric and a pinch of salt.

- For **cuts and wounds**, apply a paste of turmeric and water directly to the affected area for its antibacterial properties.

- For **arthritis relief,** take turmeric supplements or incorporate more turmeric into your meals daily.

- For **digestive problems, add** turmeric regularly to your meals or drink turmeric tea to improve digestion.

- To treat **acne**, apply a paste of turmeric and honey to the affected areas, leave on for 15 minutes, then rinse off.

- If you suffer from **diabetes,** incorporating turmeric into your daily diet could help regulate your blood sugar levels.

TURMERIC IN COOKING

Turmeric rice

INGREDIENTS: 1 cup basmati rice, 2 cups water, 1 tsp turmeric powder, 1 tbsp olive oil, 1 tsp salt, fresh coriander (optional).

1. Rinse the rice in cold water until the water runs clear.

2. In a saucepan, heat the olive oil and add the turmeric powder. Stir for a minute.

3. Add the rice and mix well to coat with turmeric.

4. Add 2 cups water and salt. Bring to a boil.

5. Reduce the heat, cover and simmer for 18 minutes, or until the rice is tender and the water absorbed.

6. Serve hot, garnished with fresh coriander if you like. Enjoy this colorful, fragrant dish!

CINNAMON

(Cinnamomum verum)

FOR A TOUCH OF SPICE AND SWEETNESS

Now let's discover cinnamon, a spice of ancient origins universally appreciated for its distinctive taste and numerous therapeutic virtues, which takes us on an unforgettable gustatory and olfactory journey.

Cinnamon, derived from the inner bark of several species of tree in the Lauraceae family, has a rich and fascinating history, dating back to ancient Egypt. It was a highly prized spice in antiquity, often more expensive than gold, used for embalming and as a divine offering. The Greeks and Romans worshipped it to perfume their clothes and drinks. It has crossed eras and continents, being a crucial element in the spice trade between Asia, Africa and Europe. In the Middle Ages, cinnamon was valued for its medicinal properties, and in the 17th century, it was the epicenter of numerous naval battles, such was its inestimable value. Although of Asian origin, this spice has permeated many cultures and cuisines around the world, including Mediterranean and Middle Eastern cuisine, offering warm, sweet notes to both savory and sweet dishes.

In the kitchen

Cinnamon is a versatile spice that **enhances the flavor of** many sweet and savory dishes. It is best known for its use in pastries, fruit compotes and hot drinks such as cider and chai. But cinnamon doesn't just add flavor; it also possesses **antioxidant, anti-inflammatory and antimicrobial properties**. It is often used to improve **digestion** and can help **regulate blood sugar levels, which** is particularly beneficial for people with type 2 diabetes. In traditional medicine, it has also been credited with **improving blood circulation** and for its **warming effect**, particularly appreciated during the winter months. The use of cinnamon in cooking is not just a question of taste; incorporating this spice into your daily diet can also contribute to a healthy lifestyle. It goes wonderfully well with fruits such as apples and pears, flavors stews and curries nicely, and can even be added to meat marinades, bringing a spicy-sweet note that balances out flavors. In short, cinnamon is a treasure trove of aromas and benefits that deserves a place of choice in every kitchen.

HEALING WITH CINNAMON

- To **regulate blood sugar levels**, take half a teaspoon of powdered cinnamon with a tablespoon of honey every day before breakfast.

- For **colds**, make cinnamon tea by adding a cinnamon stick to boiling water. Leave to infuse for 10 minutes, then drink. This can also relieve **sore throats**.

- To relieve **menstrual pain**, mix a teaspoon of powdered cinnamon in a cup of hot water. Drink this mixture three times a day.

- For **fungal infections**, apply a paste of powdered cinnamon and water to the affected area.

- If you have **digestive problems,** mix a teaspoon of cinnamon powder in a cup of hot milk and drink before bed.

- To treat **acne and blemishes**, make a paste with powdered cinnamon and honey and apply to the affected areas.

- For **headaches,** inhale cinnamon essential oil diluted in hot water.

CINNAMON IN THE KITCHEN

Cinnamon Cookies

INGREDIENTS: 200 g flour, 100 g butter, 100 g sugar, 1 egg, 1 tsp cinnamon powder, 1 tsp baking powder, 1 pinch salt.

1. Preheat your oven to 180°C.

2. Mix the dry ingredients in a bowl.

3. Add the butter and mix to a sandy consistency.

4. Stir in the egg to form a smooth dough.

5. Form small balls of dough and place on a baking sheet lined with parchment paper.

6. Bake for 12-15 minutes or until golden brown.

7. Cool on a wire rack before serving.

CARDAMOM

(Elettaria cardamomum)

AN ORIENTAL AROMATIC QUEEN

Let's head east to discover an exquisite, aromatic spice: cardamom, renowned for its heady fragrance and numerous therapeutic virtues.

Cardamom, sometimes called the "queen of spices", is native to the Indian subcontinent. It has been used since ancient times in traditional cooking and medicine for its medicinal properties and unique, aromatic taste. Cardamom seeds are known for their digestive benefits and are used to flavor teas and coffees in many countries, notably in the Middle East. They are contained in small green capsules that open when the seeds are mature. Cardamom was brought to Europe by the Greeks in the 4th century B.C. after their travels in East Asia, and was highly prized by the Romans for its digestive properties and refreshing aroma. The Vikings discovered cardamom during their expeditions to Constantinople in the 10th century and introduced it to Scandinavia, where it remains a spice of choice, particularly in pastries. Its richness in essential oils and its anti-inflammatory and antispasmodic properties make it invaluable for treating a variety of ailments such as indigestion, bloating, constipation and even headaches and migraines.

In the kitchen

Cardamom is a culinary treasure, delicately perfuming dishes, desserts, teas and coffees. **Fragrant and aromatic**, it balances and enhances flavors, bringing a sweet and spicy note to a multitude of recipes. This spice is particularly appreciated in Indian and Middle Eastern cuisine, where it is often used in spice blends such as garam masala and masala chai. Cardamom is ideal for **spicing up sweet and savory dishes**, and is a key spice in Scandinavian pastries and flavored hot drinks. **Antioxidant and digestive**, it combines perfectly with ingredients such as chocolate, apple and orange in desserts, while adding a spicy touch to meat and vegetable dishes. It goes well with other spices such as cinnamon, cloves and black pepper. Cardamom is **invaluable for digestion**, soothing indigestion, bloating and gastric pain. It is also useful for freshening breath, which is why it is often found in Asia as an ingredient in chewing gum and other confectionery.

To take full advantage of its benefits and flavor, it is advisable to grind cardamom seeds freshly to preserve its powerful aroma and medicinal properties. Be careful how you use it, however, as its taste is quite strong and can overpower other flavors in a dish if used in large quantities.

CURE YOURSELF WITH CARDAMOM

- To combat **bad breath,** chew a few cardamom seeds.

- For **bloating**, make a tea with 1 teaspoon of crushed cardamom seeds in a cup of boiling water. Leave to infuse for 10 minutes, then drink.

- For **headaches,** infuse 2 teaspoons of cardamom seeds in a cup of hot water for 15 minutes and drink.

- For **urinary tract infections,** drink a decoction of cardamom seeds regularly.

- To relieve **heartburn,** chew a cardamom seed slowly.

- For **coughs,** prepare a mixture of honey and cardamom powder and take a teaspoonful when needed.

- To treat **skin problems** such as acne, prepare a mask with cardamom powder mixed with rosewater and apply to affected areas.

CARDAMOM IN THE KITCHEN

Rice pudding with cardamom

INGREDIENTS: 100g rice, 1L milk, 100g sugar, 6 green cardamom pods, a few pistachios for garnish.

1. Rinse the rice in cold water.

2. Bring the milk to the boil with the opened cardamom pods.

3. Add the rice and sugar to the boiling milk.

4. Cook over a low heat for about 30 minutes, until the rice is tender.

5. Then remove the cardamom capsules.

6. Pour the rice pudding into bowls and garnish with pistachios.

7. Serve hot or cold and enjoy this delicious, aromatic dessert.

CLOVES
(Syzygium aromaticum)

AN ALLY FOR ORAL HEALTH

Cloves, known for their antiseptic properties, take us on a journey to the Indonesian archipelagos, where their warm, spicy aroma makes them a mainstay of gastronomy and traditional medicine.

Cloves have a rich history, closely linked to that of the spice trade. Originally from the Moluccan Islands in Indonesia, it was already used in China in the 3rd century BC. The Chinese chewed it to freshen their breath before addressing the emperor. Its use spread throughout Asia, the Middle East and then Europe, during trade. It was a precious commodity, even leading to wars over control of its production. Cloves have long been used for their medicinal properties, including antiseptic, anti-inflammatory and anesthetic properties, particularly appreciated in dentistry for soothing toothache. Today, cloves are available all over the world, being not only a spice appreciated for its unique flavor, but also a natural remedy for various ailments, such as digestive problems and infections. It is also a key ingredient in various perfumes and personal care products, thanks to its distinctive, powerful aroma.

In the kitchen

Cloves are a staple of **gastronomy the world over**, adding a warm, spicy touch to many dishes. It is particularly appreciated in sweet preparations such as cookies, cakes and compotes, where its intense fragrance **enhances the flavors**. But it's equally at home in savory dishes, such as marinades, braised meats and stews. Its penetrating flavor and woody aroma can **balance and enrich** dishes, while adding a warm, spicy note. But beware, it is powerful, so use sparingly to avoid overpowering the other flavors in the dish. In addition to its presence in cooking, clove is **rich in antioxidants**, making it beneficial to health. It can help fight infection, improve digestion and reduce inflammation. Clove infusions are also appreciated for their **antiseptic and anti-inflammatory properties**, especially for sore throats. So when you use cloves in cooking, you benefit not only from their taste, but also from their health benefits.

HEALING WITH CLOVES

- For **toothaches,** place a clove near the painful tooth until the pain subsides. You can also use a few drops of clove essential oil.

- For **digestive problems,** chew a few cloves after meals. This aids digestion and combats bloating and flatulence.

- For a **sore throat,** make an infusion with a few cloves and honey, and gargle with it. This will relieve pain and reduce inflammation.

- If you suffer from **acne,** apply clove essential oil diluted in a vegetable oil to the affected areas. This will help reduce inflammation and acne-causing bacteria.

- For **skin infections**, apply an ointment containing clove oil to the infected area for antiseptic action.

- For **mental fatigue,** inhale the aroma of clove essential oil to stimulate the mind and reduce fatigue.

CLOVES IN COOKING

Rice Pilaf with Cloves

INGREDIENTS: 300 g basmati rice, 1 onion, 2 garlic cloves, 5 cloves, 1 cinnamon stick, 600 ml vegetable stock, 1 tbsp olive oil, salt and pepper.

1. Peel and finely chop the onion and garlic.

2. Heat the oil in a saucepan and sauté the onion, garlic, cloves and cinnamon for 2 minutes.

3. Add the rice and stir well to allow it to absorb the aromas.

4. Pour in the hot stock, season with salt and pepper, then bring to the boil.

5. Reduce the heat, cover and simmer for 15-20 minutes, until the rice is tender and has absorbed the liquid.

6. Remove cloves and cinnamon before serving. Enjoy hot.

CORIANDER
(Coriandrum sativum)

A condiment for the heart and mind Explore the world of spices with coriander, a culinary and medicinal herb with deep roots in cultures around the globe.

 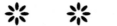

Native to regions ranging from southern Europe to western Asia, coriander is a condiment that has crossed continents and civilizations. Its seeds have been found in ancient Egyptian tombs, underlining its ancient use in both cooking and medicine.

Known since antiquity to the Greeks and Romans as a culinary ingredient and remedy, coriander is cited in various ancient texts, including the Bible. Doctors of the time, such as Hippocrates, recommended it for its medicinal properties. In China, it was believed to confer immortality, and in the Middle Ages, it was used to combat the unpleasant smell of rotting meat. Today, it is an essential ingredient in a variety of cuisines, including Asian, Latin American and Middle Eastern, thanks to its distinctive aroma and numerous culinary applications.

In the kitchen

Coriander is an **essential element in many of the world's cuisines**, offering a refreshing, lemony flavor. The leaves and seeds are used to **add a touch of freshness and piquancy** to dishes. Coriander seeds are **beneficial for digestion** and are often used in spice blends for curries, soups and stews.

The leaves, also known as cilantro, are **rich in vitamins A, C and K,** and are commonly used as a garnish in Mexican and Indian dishes. Coriander essential oil, extracted from the seeds, is a popular addition to **flavor foods and beverages**. In addition to its culinary uses, coriander is also **prized in phytotherapy** for its digestive, antispasmodic and **antibacterial** properties.

Coriander isn't just a taste enhancer; it's a **natural** way to **boost the immune system** and **promote digestive health,** thanks to its active components such as linoleic acids, oleic acids and palmitic acid.

CURE YOURSELF WITH CORIANDER

- To improve digestion and relieve flatulence, make an herbal tea with a teaspoon of ground coriander seeds in a cup of boiling water. Leave to infuse for 5-10 minutes, then strain and drink.

- For a sore throat, gargle with a decoction of coriander seeds (one teaspoon of seeds to a glass of water) three times a day.

- For skin infections, apply a paste made from crushed coriander leaves to the affected area.

- If you have eye problems such as conjunctivitis, eyewashes with coriander decoction can be soothing.

- To combat pimples and blemishes, mix a drop of coriander essential oil in a teaspoon of coconut oil and apply locally.

CORIANDER IN THE KITCHEN

Coriander salsa

INGREDIENTS: 3 tomatoes, 1 onion, 1 garlic clove, 1 chili pepper, 1 bunch coriander, juice of 1 lime, salt and pepper.

- Finely chop the tomatoes, onion, garlic, green pepper and coriander.

- Mix in a bowl with the lime juice.

- Add salt and pepper to taste.

- Let the salsa stand for about 30 minutes before serving to allow the flavours to blend. Enjoy with corn chips or as an accompaniment to your favorite dishes!

CUMIN
(Cuminum cyminum)

A STAR OF ORIENTAL CUISINE

Let's continue our gastronomic and medicinal journey around the world with cumin, a rich, fragrant spice from the Middle East, much appreciated for its many therapeutic virtues and warm, earthy aromas.

Cumin, one of the most popular spices, has been used for thousands of years. Native to the Middle East, it was mentioned in the Bible and used in ancient Egypt, both in cooking and for mummification. It is an annual plant of the Apiaceae family, growing mainly in warm regions such as India, Mexico, China and the Mediterranean. Cumin seeds are prized for their distinctive spicy and bitter taste, and are often used in Indian, Mexican and Middle Eastern cuisine. The spice was introduced to America by Spanish and

Portuguese colonists. Cumin was considered a symbol of love and fidelity, and Roman soldiers often carried cumin as provisions on their expeditions.

In the kitchen

Cumin is a fundamental element in a multitude of dishes around the world, offering a **warm**, **earthy** touch that enriches dishes. It goes particularly well with lentils, beans and meats, and is often used to prepare spice blends such as curry and garam masala. In addition, cumin has an array of **medicinal properties**: it is rich in iron and beneficial to digestion, **stimulating the production of bile**, making it ideal for seasoning rich, fatty dishes. It is also reputed to **relieve digestive disorders** such as bloating, cramps and gas. The presence of bioactive compounds in cumin also makes it a **powerful antioxidant**, protecting cells against free radical damage and fortifying the immune system. What's more, its wealth of essential oils gives it **antibacterial and anti-inflammatory** properties. In traditional medicine, cumin is often used to treat respiratory problems, insomnia and certain skin conditions, and modern research is beginning to validate some of these traditional uses, underlining the importance of this spice both in cooking and for general well-being. It is also an important source of **iron**, essential for oxygen transport in the blood, making it an ally in the fight against anemia. By using cumin in cooking, we can therefore enjoy not only exquisite flavours but also health benefits.

CURE YOURSELF WITH CUMIN

- For **difficult digestion**, mix a teaspoon of cumin seeds in hot water and leave to infuse for 5-10 minutes. Drink this tea after meals to aid digestion.

- To **soothe stomach cramps,** chew a teaspoon of cumin seeds.

- If you have **gas problems,** take a teaspoon of cumin seeds with honey after meals.

- For **coughs,** mix a pinch of ground cumin with a teaspoon of honey. Take 2-3 times a day.

- For **colds and sinusitis,** inhale a teaspoon of cumin seeds in boiling water.

- For **acne**, create a paste with powdered cumin and water and apply to affected areas. Leave on for 30 minutes, then rinse off.

- If you suffer from **insomnia,** consume a mixture of cumin powder and a banana before going to bed.

CUMIN IN COOKING

Rice with Cumin

INGREDIENTS: 1 cup basmati rice, 2 tsp cumin seeds, 1 finely chopped onion, 2 tbsp olive oil, 2 cups water, salt to taste.

1. Heat the oil in a saucepan and add the cumin seeds. Fry until they begin to crackle.

2. Add the chopped onion and sauté until golden.

3. Add the rice and stir well to coat the grains with oil and cumin.

4. Add water and salt and bring to the boil.

5. Reduce the heat, cover and simmer for 18 minutes, or until the water is absorbed and the rice is tender.

6. Serve hot and enjoy your cumin rice!

STAR ANISE

(Illicium verum)

THE SCENT OF A STAR IN THE KITCHEN

Let's continue our aromatic journey to the Far East, to discover star anise, a spice with a distinctive aroma and recognized medicinal properties that captivates the senses and awakens the taste buds.

Star anise, often called star anise, is a spice native to China. It has been used through the ages, both for its medicinal properties and for its unique taste and powerful aroma. This spice is the fruit of the evergreen Illicium verum. The fruit is harvested before ripening and then dried, giving it its characteristic star shape. Used since ancient times in China and India for its health benefits, star anise was also adopted in traditional Persian medicine. Star anise first appeared in Europe in the 17th century, introduced by the English explorer Sir Thomas Cavendish. Today, it remains a popular spice in many cuisines, and its medicinal benefits are widely recognized and studied.

In the kitchen

Star anise is prized for its licorice-like flavor and spicy-sweet aroma, and is a perfect complement to sweet and savory dishes, particularly duck and pork. It is also an essential component of spice blends such as Chinese five-spice. It is also frequently used to make hot drinks and liqueurs. In addition to its culinary uses, star anise is rich in **antioxidants** and possesses **antifungal** and **anti-inflammatory** properties. It has been shown to **aid digestion** and can help **fight viral infections**, thanks in particular to its shikimic acid content, a compound used in the manufacture of anti-flu drugs. Star anise is also reputed to **relieve stomach upset** and bloating, and is often used in traditional medicine to treat respiratory disorders such as coughs and asthma. However, it's crucial to note that only Chinese star anise (Illicium verum) is edible, its Japanese counterpart (Illicium anisatum) being toxic. In short, whether for flavoring dishes or for its many health benefits, star anise is a rising star in the world of spices.

HEALING WITH STAR ANISE

- To relieve **bloating**, prepare an infusion with a star of anise in a cup of boiling water. Leave to infuse for 10 minutes and drink after meals.

- For **colds and flu,** make a decoction of star anise. Add one star to a cup of boiling water and drink the mixture 2-3 times a day.

- **For digestive** problems, chew a star after a meal or prepare an infusion to improve digestion.

- For **headaches,** inhale star anise essential oil diluted in hot water.

- For **menstrual pain**, make a tea with a star of star anise and drink it hot 2-3 times a day.

- For **insomnia,** have a cup of star anise tea before bedtime.

- If you suffer from a **sore throat,** gargle with an infusion of star anise several times a day.

STAR ANISE IN THE KITCHEN

Star Anise Cookies

INGREDIENTS: 200 g flour, 100 g sugar, 100 g butter, 1 egg, 1 tsp baking powder, 1 tbsp ground star anise seeds.

1. Preheat oven to 180°C.

2. Mix flour, sugar, butter, egg, baking powder and star anise in a bowl until smooth.

3. Shape small balls of dough and place on a baking sheet lined with parchment paper.

4. Bake for 12-15 minutes or until golden brown.

5. Cool on a wire rack before serving. Enjoy your star anise cookies!

FENNEL
(FOENICULUM VULGARE)

FOR A TOUCH OF MEDITERRANEAN FRESHNESS

*Fennel, with its aniseed flavor and crunchy texture,
takes us on a Mediterranean journey, combining
gustatory pleasures with health benefits.*

Originally from the Mediterranean basin, fennel has
been appreciated since ancient times for its many medicinal
and culinary virtues. The Greeks adored it for its ability to
increase endurance and strength, and the Romans valued it
for its beneficial properties for eyesight. Fennel, with its
crisp stems and tender green leaves, is an aromatic plant
with a sweet, refreshing aniseed aroma. It's rich in vitamin
C, fiber, potassium and other essential minerals. This
vegetable, or rather herb, has crossed the ages, civilizations
and continents, incorporating itself deliciously into various
cuisines while retaining its reputation as a valuable

medicinal plant. Whether in Italy, India or the Middle East, every culture has adopted and adapted fennel to its culinary and medicinal traditions, making this versatile plant an undisputed star in the world of aromatic and medicinal plants.

In the kitchen

Fennel is a fantastic cooking ingredient, renowned for its distinctive flavor and **digestive properties**. It can be enjoyed raw, grilled, braised or steamed, adding a refreshing crunch to salads and an aniseed-like sweetness to hot dishes. Used to enhance fish, meat or vegetarian dishes, fennel has the gift of transforming a simple recipe into a sophisticated, fragrant dish. Its **high fiber content** makes it ideal for digestive health, and its **vitamin C content** makes it an ally for the immune system. **Fennel seeds are** also highly prized, especially for making digestive herbal teas, as they aid digestion and help relieve bloating and abdominal cramps. Fennel essential oil is used for its **antispasmodic and anti-inflammatory properties**, particularly to soothe menstrual pain. In many cultures, chewing fennel seeds is a common practice after meals, not only to freshen breath but also to aid digestion. Finally, this Mediterranean vegetable has found its way into many culinary preparations, from soups and stews to gratins and breads, offering a multitude of ways to enjoy its benefits and unique taste.

HEALING WITH FENNEL

- For **indigestion,** infuse a teaspoon of fennel seeds in a cup of boiling water for 10 minutes, then strain and drink the tea up to three times a day.

- For **respiratory problems**, inhale steam from a decoction of fennel leaves to help clear the airways.

- For **eye congestion,** apply a fennel poultice to the eyes.

- To relieve **menstrual pain,** drink fennel seed tea several times a day.

- If you suffer from **bloating,** chew half a teaspoon of fennel seeds after meals.

- For **gum inflammation,** rinse your mouth with a decoction of fennel.

- For **irritated skin**, apply fennel essential oil diluted in a vegetable oil to the affected area for its soothing, anti-inflammatory properties.

FENNEL IN THE KITCHEN

Crunchy Fennel Salad

INGREDIENTS: 1 fennel bulb, 2 tbsp olive oil, 1 tbsp lemon juice, salt, pepper, a handful of chopped fresh parsley, 50 g grated Parmesan cheese.

1. Wash and finely chop the fennel bulb.

2. In a salad bowl, combine the chopped fennel, olive oil, lemon juice, salt and pepper.

3. Leave to marinate for about 15 minutes.

4. Add chopped parsley and grated Parmesan before serving.

5. Adjust seasoning if necessary and serve chilled. Enjoy this crunchy fennel salad as a refreshing starter or as an accompaniment to a main course.

BLACK PEPPER
(PIPER NIGRUM)

A TREASURE TROVE OF WORLD GASTRONOMY

Black pepper, renowned for its pungent flavor and intense aroma, is a staple of cuisines the world over and is often referred to as the "king of spices".

Originating from the Malabar coast of India, black pepper is one of the oldest and most widely traded spices in the world. Used by the Greeks and Romans as a currency of exchange, it was worth its weight in gold. The pepper trade played a major role in shaping the maritime trade routes between India, the Middle East, Europe and North Africa. The discovery of new sea routes to India in the 15th century was largely motivated by the desire for direct access to pepper sources. Pepper's use rapidly spread throughout the world's cuisines, not only for its gustatory qualities but also for its medicinal virtues. Rich in piperine, a molecule with anti-inflammatory and antioxidant properties, black pepper has been used since ancient times to treat various ailments such as digestive disorders, inflammation and certain infections.

In the kitchen

Black pepper is ubiquitous in the kitchen, enhancing both savory and sweet dishes. It adds **a** uniquely **spicy and aromatic flavor**, appreciated in cuisines the world over. Used as a grain or ground, it blends harmoniously with a multitude of ingredients. It's a true ally for **enhancing the flavors of** meats, fish, seafood, sauces, soups and even certain desserts and beverages. It has become so commonplace that its **digestive properties** are often overlooked. Black pepper stimulates the production of gastric juices, facilitating digestion. It also has **antibacterial properties** that can help fight food-borne infections. In the culinary arts, black pepper is used not only for its gustatory qualities, but also for its ability to **enhance the bioavailability** of certain nutrients and phytochemicals, making foods even more beneficial to health. However, although common, it should be used in moderation, as its dominant taste can easily overshadow other flavors in a dish. Ultimately, black pepper is a versatile treasure that enriches our palates and our lives, making everyday meals extraordinary.

HEALING WITH BLACK PEPPER

- To **improve digestion**, take half a teaspoon of ground black pepper, mix it in a glass of lukewarm water with a teaspoon of honey and drink this mixture once a day.

- For **colds and congestion,** mix a pinch of ground black pepper into a cup of ginger tea. This will help clear the airways and relieve congestion.

- To **relieve coughs,** take a teaspoon of honey mixed with a pinch of ground black pepper, two or three times a day.

- For **headaches,** inhale steam from boiling water mixed with a teaspoon of black peppercorns, to help open nasal passages and relieve tension.

- To **reduce skin inflammation**, mix a pinch of ground black pepper with coconut oil and apply locally.

- For **indigestion,** mix a pinch of black pepper with a teaspoon of cumin seeds and salt, and drink with water.

- If you suffer from **toothache,** make a mouthwash with a solution of ground black pepper and salt in lukewarm water.

BLACK PEPPER IN COOKING

Black Pepper Steak

INGREDIENTS: 2 steaks, 2 tbsp crushed black peppercorns, 1 tbsp olive oil, 1 tsp salt, 100 ml crème fraîche, 50 ml cognac or brandy.

1. Season steaks with salt and press crushed black peppercorns onto each side.

2. Heat the oil in a frying pan and cook the steaks to your liking.

3. Remove the steaks and add the cognac to the pan. Cook over high heat to reduce by half.

4. Add the cream and stir well. Cook for a few more minutes until the sauce thickens slightly.

5. Pour the sauce over the steaks and serve immediately. Enjoy your meal!

PAPRIKA

FOR A SMOKY, SPICY FLAVOR

*Let's embark on a new stage of our epicurean journey
and discover paprika, that vibrant red spice synonymous
with warmth and convivial cuisine, often associated with
Hungarian and Spanish gastronomy.*

Originally from South America, paprika was introduced
to Europe by Spanish explorers in the 16th century. It
became a central ingredient in many cuisines, notably
Hungarian and Spanish. Paprika is obtained by drying and
grinding certain types of chili pepper or red bell pepper.
Paprika varieties can vary in taste, from sweet to spicy, and
in color, from orange-yellow to deep red. In Hungary,
paprika is not only a culinary condiment, but also a national
symbol of pride and tradition. Paprika is also essential in
the manufacture of certain sausages and cold meats. In
traditional medicine, it is used for its anti-inflammatory and

circulatory properties, as well as to stimulate the appetite and aid digestion. Paprika is rich in vitamin C and other antioxidants, making it a valuable ally in combating free radicals and supporting the immune system. It also has a thermogenic effect, promoting weight loss.

In the kitchen

Paprika is a chameleon in the kitchen. **Enhancing the** flavor and color of dishes, it's a friend of stews, soups, eggs and grilled meats. It adds a unique **depth and warmth**, ideal for enhancing bland dishes. Smoked paprika adds a special flavor to fish and seafood dishes. In Spanish paella, it **contributes** to the characteristic taste that everyone loves. What's more, paprika is a **powerful antioxidant** and, thanks to its high vitamin A content, **promotes** healthy eyes. Its distinctive taste and vibrant color make paprika a decorative and tasty addition to salads, potatoes and cheeses. Combined with salt and garlic, it makes an excellent rub for meats before cooking. Not only does paprika add **warmth and richness** to a variety of dishes, it **also intensifies nutritional benefits**, adding essential vitamins and minerals. It's a condiment that finds a place in almost any dish, offering a **perfect balance** between flavor and health benefits. Beware, however, of paprika's heat; a small amount is often enough to spice up a dish.

HEALING WITH PAPRIKA

- For **digestive problems,** a teaspoon of paprika in soup or broth can aid digestion.

- For **inflammatory pain,** mix half a teaspoon of paprika with hot water and drink the mixture once a day.

- To support **visual health,** regularly add paprika to your dishes. It's rich in vitamin A, which is good for the eyes.

- To boost **metabolism and weight loss**, add a pinch of paprika to your dishes. It has a thermogenic effect that can help burn calories.

- For **colds,** sprinkle paprika in your soups. It helps clear the respiratory tract and reduce congestion.

- If you have **skin infections,** apply a paste of paprika and water to the affected area. Its antiseptic effect can help healing.

PAPRIKA IN THE KITCHEN

Paprika Goulash

INGREDIENTS: 500 g diced beef, 2 tbsp olive oil, 2 chopped onions, 2 crushed garlic cloves, 2 tbsp paprika, 400 g diced tomatoes, 500 ml beef stock, salt and pepper.

1. Heat the oil in a saucepan and brown the beef until golden brown. Remove from the pan.

2. In the same pan, sauté the onions and garlic until tender.

3. Add the paprika and sauté for one minute.

4. Return the beef to the pan, add the tomatoes and stock. Season with salt and pepper.

5. Bring to the boil, reduce heat and simmer for about 2 hours, or until beef is tender. Serve hot and enjoy!

NUTMEG
(MYRISTICA FRAGRANS)

FOR A SWEET FRAGRANCE AND SURPRISING BENEFITS

Let's continue our spicy journey to the islands of the Indonesian archipelago, home to nutmeg, an emblematic spice that delights our senses and enlivens our dishes with its distinctive aroma and warm, sweet taste.

Nutmeg, the famous spice from the island of Banda, was long a well-kept secret among the islanders before it reached the rest of the world in the early Middle Ages. The Romans and Greeks valued it for its medicinal and aromatic properties. During the Middle Ages, the Arabs introduced it to Europe, where it became particularly prized, symbolizing luxury and exoticism. The nutmeg trade was jealously guarded, and was at the heart of fierce battles between colonial powers for control of the Banda islands. Today, nutmeg is accessible to all, and is used both in cooking and for its many health benefits. This spice, derived from the fruit of the nutmeg tree, has a unique flavor, both sweet and intense, with notes of pine and camphor.

In the kitchen

Nutmeg is a versatile spice that adds **depth and warmth** to a multitude of dishes. It is often used to **enhance the flavor of purées, bechamels and desserts.** Its **suave, spicy aroma is a** must in winter cooking, especially in hot drinks like eggnog. But nutmeg is not only appreciated for its unique flavor, it also possesses **antispasmodic and anti-inflammatory properties. Indeed,** it is often used to relieve **joint pain** and **digestive problems** such as bloating and constipation. Simply grate a little of this spice over your dishes to enjoy its benefits. Nutmeg also acts as a **natural** food **preservative,** thanks to its antibacterial properties. Nutmeg has an important place in traditional medicine for treating various disorders such as insomnia and anxiety, thanks to its soothing effect on the nervous system. However, it must be consumed in moderation, as large quantities can be toxic. Excessive consumption of nutmeg can lead to symptoms such as nausea, hallucinations and dehydration. All in all, nutmeg, used judiciously, can be an excellent addition to health and cooking.

HEALING WITH NUTMEG

- To relieve **joint pain**, mix a pinch of powdered nutmeg with a little water to form a paste. Apply this paste to painful areas.

- For **indigestion,** take a pinch of powdered nutmeg mixed with a teaspoon of honey before eating.

- To combat **insomnia,** mix a pinch of nutmeg powder with a glass of warm milk before bedtime.

- If you have a **toothache,** apply a pinch of powdered nutmeg to the affected area.

- To treat **skin infections**, apply a nutmeg paste to the affected area several times a day.

- For **headaches,** inhale the aroma of diluted nutmeg essential oil.

- If you suffer from an **upset stomach,** drink an infusion of nutmeg. Brew half a teaspoon of grated nutmeg in hot water for 10 minutes and drink twice a day.

NUTMEG IN THE KITCHEN

Mashed potatoes with nutmeg

INGREDIENTS: 1 kg potatoes, 50 g butter, 200 ml milk, salt, pepper, 1/2 tsp grated nutmeg.

1. Peel and chop the potatoes. Cook in a pot of boiling salted water until tender.

2. Drain the potatoes and mash with a potato masher or fork.

3. Heat the milk and butter in a saucepan until the butter has melted.

4. Gradually add the milk and butter mixture to the mashed potatoes, mixing well to obtain a smooth purée.

5. Season with salt, pepper and grated nutmeg.

6. Serve the hot nutmeg mashed potatoes as a side dish. Enjoy!

SAFFRON
(CROCUS SATIVUS)

THE RED GOLD OF SPICES

Let's take off for an even more exotic destination, rich in spices, to discover saffron, nicknamed "red gold", an ingredient with a unique taste and multiple benefits.

Saffron is a spice derived from the flower of the Crocus sativus plant, cultivated since ancient times in Greece and Asia Minor. It is one of the most expensive spices in the world, due to the difficulty of harvesting it. It takes around 150,000 flowers to produce one kilo of saffron! Saffron has been used throughout history as a seasoning, food coloring and medicine. Its medicinal properties, notably anti-inflammatory and antioxidant, were already known to Greek physicians. In traditional Indian and Chinese medicine, it is used to treat a wide range of ailments, including depression and inflammation. Saffron is also associated with spirituality, and is often used in religious rituals.

In the kitchen

Saffron is a culinary treasure. It **enhances dishes** with a subtle flavor and gives them a beautiful golden hue. It is particularly appreciated in Spanish paella, Italian risottos, and certain Indian and Persian dishes. But that's not all: in addition to its **unique aroma**, saffron has **significant medicinal properties**. Rich in antioxidants, it **fights free radicals**, **protects against heart disease**, and improves **memory and concentration**. It is also **effective against inflammation** and helps **combat depression**. All in all, saffron is a versatile spice that combines flavor, color and health benefits. However, due to its high price, it is often used sparingly. Saffron is also a very fragile spice, so store it in a cool, dry, dark place to preserve its taste and properties.

HEALING WITH SAFFRON

- To **improve mood and combat depression**, infuse a few saffron filaments in a cup of hot water. Drink this infusion once or twice a day.

- For **sleep disorders,** use saffron as an infusion or add it to food to help improve sleep quality.

- To **relieve PMS symptoms**, infuse a few saffron filaments in water and drink the decoction.

- For **skin problems** such as pimples and pigmentation spots, apply a mixture of saffron infused in water or milk to the skin.

- For **memory loss,** include saffron in your diet on a regular basis. Saffron is known for its **memory-enhancing** properties.

- For **pain** and inflammation, a saffron infusion can be taken regularly.

- If you suffer from **digestive problems,** use saffron as a spice in your dishes. It helps **improve digestion** and relieve **intestinal gas**.

SAFFRON IN THE KITCHEN

Saffron Risotto

INGREDIENTS: 320 g Arborio rice, 1 onion, 100 ml white wine, 1 L hot vegetable stock, a pinch of saffron filaments, 30 g butter, 40 g grated Parmesan cheese, salt, pepper.

1. Infuse the saffron filaments in a little hot stock.

2. In a frying pan, melt the butter and sauté the chopped onion until transparent.

3. Add the rice and sauté until pearly.

4. Moisten with white wine and allow to evaporate.

5. Add the hot broth and saffron infusion, stirring
    continuously, until the rice is cooked.

6. Remove from the heat, add the grated Parmesan
    and adjust the seasoning with salt and pepper if
    necessary. Serve hot and enjoy!

CAYENNE PEPPER
(CAPSICUM ANNUUM)

TASTY, THERAPEUTIC FIRE

Discover cayenne pepper, a condiment that comes from a variety of hot pepper native to a region of South America. Known for its fiery taste, this spice also has many medicinal virtues.

Cayenne pepper, native to the Cayenne region of French Guiana, is a spice famous for its heat and pungent flavor, used in cuisines around the world to spice up dishes. This small red or green pepper, which belongs to the Solanaceae family, was introduced to Europe by Christopher Columbus in the 15th century. It is said to have been first cultivated and consumed in the Cayenne region, hence its name. It is an annual tropical plant that is now cultivated in many tropical and subtropical regions of the world. Cayenne pepper has a long history of use both as a spice and as a medicine. Traditional physicians have used it for centuries to treat a variety of ailments, from digestive disorders to blood circulation problems. The indigenous peoples of South America also used cayenne pepper to treat pain and inflammation. Its medicinal properties are mainly attributed to a compound called capsaicin, which is also responsible for its fiery flavor.

In the kitchen

Cayenne pepper is widely used in cooking to add a **spicy, hot flavor** to dishes. It can be used in powder form to season meats, stews and sauces, or in sauce form to accompany a variety of dishes. It is a key ingredient in many of the world's cuisines, including Mexican, Creole, Asian and Indian. Cayenne pepper is renowned not only for its distinctive **hot taste, but** also for its **medicinal properties**. It is known to **stimulate digestion, improve blood circulation** and **speed up metabolism**, which can aid weight loss. In addition, it has **anti-inflammatory and analgesic properties, which** can be beneficial in reducing pain and inflammation. Cayenne pepper can be an excellent addition to your dishes, not only to enhance flavor, but also to reap its many health benefits. However, it should be used in moderation, as its flavor is very intense and can irritate the digestive system in some people.

CURE YOURSELF WITH CAYENNE PEPPER

* To relieve **joint pain**, mix a teaspoon of cayenne powder in a cup of coconut oil or olive oil and apply to painful areas.

- For **difficult digestion,** take a small pinch of cayenne powder in a glass of warm water before meals to stimulate digestion.

- To **combat colds**, add half a teaspoon of cayenne powder to a cup of hot water with honey and lemon. Drink this infusion 2-3 times a day.

- For a **sore throat**, gargle with a solution of half a teaspoon of cayenne powder dissolved in a glass of lukewarm water.

- If you suffer from **migraines,** an infusion of cayenne pepper can help, thanks to its anti-inflammatory properties.

- For **skin problems such as acne**, create a mask with cayenne powder and water and apply locally. Caution: test on a small area of skin first to avoid irritation.

CAYENNE PEPPER IN COOKING

Cayenne Hot Sauce

INGREDIENTS: 2 tbsp cayenne pepper powder, 1 cup apple cider vinegar, 1 tsp salt, 2 tbsp tomato purée, 1 clove garlic, minced.

1. Mix all ingredients in a saucepan.

2. Bring to the boil, then reduce heat and simmer for about 15-20 minutes.

3. Once the sauce has reduced and thickened, remove from the heat and allow to cool.

4. Pour the sauce into a sterilized bottle and store in the fridge. Use this sauce to spice up your dishes and enjoy the intense, spicy flavor of cayenne pepper. Caution: this sauce is very strong, so use in moderation.

VANILLA
(VANILLA PLANIFOLIA)

A SUAVE, UNMISTAKABLE AROMA

Vanilla, with its sweet, distinctive aroma, is one of the world's most loved and widely used spices, adding a touch of sweetness and sophistication to every dish.

Native to the tropical forests of Central America, vanilla has been known and appreciated for centuries. The Aztecs already used vanilla to flavor their chocolate, a use taken up and popularized by the Spaniards from the 16th century onwards after the conquest of America. But vanilla is fickle, and pollination is a delicate and tedious process, often carried out by hand. Mexico remained the main vanilla producer for a long time, until the plant was introduced to Réunion, Madagascar and other French colonies in the 19th century. Today, Madagascar is the world's largest vanilla producer. Vanilla comes from the fertilization of the flowers of the vanilla orchid, a painstaking process carried out by hand. It's this delicate method and the long process of ripening and drying the pods that make vanilla so precious and sought-after, the second most expensive spice after saffron.

In the kitchen

Vanilla is synonymous with sweetness in the kitchen. It **delicately perfumes creams, ice creams and cakes**, adding a unique and inimitable flavor. **Antioxidant** and rich in **phenols,** vanilla is much more than just a flavoring. In fact, it can add depth of flavor to savory dishes such as sauces and marinades. But its best-known use is in baking, where it can transform an ordinary dish into a delicious, fragrant treat. It is also used to **reduce anxiety** and improve sleep quality thanks to its soothing aroma. It is endowed with **anti-inflammatory and antioxidant** properties, which can help reduce inflammation and strengthen the immune system. In addition, its **relaxing and soothing** properties are ideal for improving mood. What's more, it has the power to **improve skin health**, thanks to its antibacterial properties. But beware, when buying, it's essential to check provenance and quality, as artificial vanilla flavours are common and don't offer the same benefits or taste as natural vanilla. So it's best to opt for good-quality whole vanilla beans or natural vanilla extract to reap the full benefits of its irresistible flavour.

HEALING WITH VANILLA

- To **soothe anxiety** and improve **sleep,** add a few drops of pure vanilla extract to a diffuser before bedtime.

- To treat **mild burns**, gently apply a few drops of vanilla essential oil mixed with a carrier oil such as coconut oil to the affected area.

- For **menstrual pain,** add a few drops of vanilla essential oil to a warm bath and relax in this aromatic bath.

- To **improve mood,** inhale the sweet, comforting aroma of vanilla straight from the extract bottle, or use a diffuser to scent a room.

- If you suffer from **skin disorders** such as acne, mix a few drops of vanilla essential oil into your day cream for its antibacterial and anti-inflammatory properties.

- To **relieve nausea,** inhale deeply the aroma of vanilla extract.

- For a **sore throat,** add a few drops of vanilla extract to a cup of hot water and gargle with this gentle, soothing mixture.

VANILLA IN THE KITCHEN

Vanilla ice cream

INGREDIENTS: 500 ml whole milk, 1 vanilla pod, 6 egg yolks, 150 g sugar, 250 ml crème fraîche.

1. Heat the milk over medium heat. Split the vanilla pod in half and scrape the seeds into the milk. Add the pod. Bring to the boil, then

remove from the heat and leave to infuse for 30 minutes.

2. Beat the egg yolks and sugar in a bowl until the mixture whitens. Remove the vanilla pod from the milk. Pour the hot milk over the egg mixture, whisking continuously.

3. Return the mixture to the pan and cook over a low heat, stirring constantly, until the cream coats the spoon.

4. Remove from the heat, allow to cool, then stir in the crème fraîche. Place the mixture in the fridge until well chilled.

5. Pour into an ice-cream maker and set according to the instructions. Then enjoy this delicious vanilla ice cream!

PART II: TRADITIONAL CHINESE PLANTS

Traditional Chinese herbs can be found on the Internet or in specialized stores. It is crucial to choose reliable suppliers to ensure the authenticity and quality of the products acquired.

GINSENG
(PANAX GINSENG)

FOR REVITALIZING ENERGY

Let's explore the depths of Eastern lands, in China and Korea, to discover a root revered for its multiple benefits: ginseng, often considered an elixir of life in traditional Eastern medicine.

The origins of ginseng go back to ancient China, where it was revered for its curative and revitalizing properties. This botanical treasure, sometimes strangely shaped like a human being, became a symbol of health, longevity and the balance of Yin and Yang. The first written accounts of its medicinal virtues date back some 5,000 years. According to legend, it could cure all kinds of ailments, strengthen Qi (vital energy), and procure immortality. It was introduced to Europe in the XVII^c century by missionaries and traders, and its use spread for its alleged ability to reduce stress and improve concentration and stamina. In Korea and China, ginseng is a valuable ingredient in cooking and medicine, used not only for its distinctive taste but also for its adaptogenic properties, helping the body adapt to stress. It is richly nutritious and known to boost energy, improve concentration and strengthen the immune system. It comes in many forms, such as fresh, dried or powdered roots, or even as a liquid extract.

In the kitchen

Ginseng is prized for its ability to infuse dishes with an earthy, sweet flavor. It is often used in soups and broths, adding not only a depth of flavor, but also a range of **health benefits**, such as improving **blood circulation** and boosting **physical and mental vitality**. A popular method is to prepare it as a tea, allowing its aromas and properties to diffuse into the water, offering a drink that is both refreshing and invigorating. Even ginseng sweets are popular in Asia, offering a nutritious sweet rich in **antioxidants** and **vitamins**. In all its culinary uses, ginseng remains a revered spice, unifying flavor, nutrition and medicine in every bite.

HEALING WITH GINSENG

- To **boost energy** and **reduce stress**, prepare a decoction by adding a chopped ginseng root to 500 ml of water. Bring to the boil and simmer for 45 minutes. Drink this decoction once or twice a day.

- For **mental fatigue,** chew a small piece of ginseng root slowly to improve **concentration and memory**.

- To **boost the immune system**, consume ginseng regularly as a dietary supplement, following the manufacturer's recommendations.

- For **sleep problems**, take a cup of ginseng tea before bedtime to improve **sleep quality**.

- To **relieve cold symptoms**, mix a teaspoon of ginseng powder in a cup of hot tea and drink.

- For **digestive problems,** consume ginseng in tea or capsule form to improve **digestion** and relieve **gastric discomfort**.

- For the **skin,** apply a cream containing ginseng extract to **revitalize** and **moisturize**.

GINSENG IN THE KITCHEN

Revitalizing ginseng soup

INGREDIENTS: 1 ginseng root, 1 whole chicken, 4 garlic cloves, 2 l water, salt and pepper to taste.

1. Cut the chicken into pieces and place in a large saucepan.

2. Add the ginseng root, garlic, salt and pepper.

3. Pour in the water and bring to the boil. Reduce heat and simmer for 1-2 hours.

4. Serve hot and enjoy this soup for energy and comfort.

ASTRAGALUS
(ASTRAGALUS MEMBRANACEUS)

NATURAL IMMUNE SYSTEM BOOSTER

*Let's discover a spice from the Orient, astragalus,
recognized for its exceptional medicinal properties,
notably as an immune system tonic and adaptogen
helping the body to combat stress.*

Native to China, astragalus is a medicinal plant that has been renowned in traditional Chinese medicine for thousands of years. It is used to strengthen vital energy (Qi) and protect the body against various illnesses. This spice, with its long stems and imparipinnate leaves, belongs to the legume family. The Chinese traditionally used astragalus to boost the immune system, prevent colds and fatigue, and treat chronic diarrhea. Once harvested and dried, astragalus roots are used to prepare decoctions, tinctures and dietary supplements. In ancient times, astragalus was also used as a general tonic to boost metabolism and digestion, improve tissue regeneration and promote healing. It was also valued as an agent of longevity and for treating chronic and inflammatory diseases. Astragalus was introduced to the West in the 19th century, where it was studied for its beneficial effects on the immune system and adaptogenic properties to combat the effects of stress.

In the kitchen

Astragalus can be used to enhance a wide range of dishes, while adding its **fortifying** and **immunostimulant properties**. It pairs well with soups and broths, where it unleashes its benefits and sweet, earthy flavor. In China, it is commonly added to chicken soups to enhance taste and provide a **nutritional boost**. In vegetarian and vegan diets, it provides **nutritional richness**, especially when combined with other medicinal plants such as ginseng. Its dried roots can be used to make health-giving teas and decoctions. This spice is particularly **rich in antioxidants**, helping to **combat oxidative stress** and **boost the immune system**. In addition to its culinary uses, astragalus is also used in natural medicine to improve **vitality** and **physical resistance,** while stimulating **digestion** and **cell regeneration**. It is crucial to cook it correctly to reap its benefits, and slow, prolonged cooking is often recommended to extract all its active components. In short, incorporating astragalus into your diet is a delicious way to enjoy its many health benefits. Beware, however, of using it with certain medications, and seek medical advice if in doubt.

HEALING WITH ASTRAGALUS

- For **chronic fatigue**, make a decoction with 1 tablespoon of dried astragalus root in 2 cups of water. Boil until reduced by half, strain and drink once a day.

- To **boost the immune system**, drink astragalus tea regularly. Add a teaspoon of dried root to a cup of boiling water and steep for 10 minutes.

- In case of **stress,** mix a few drops of astragalus extract in a drink or smoothie and consume daily.

- For **skin problems**, apply a paste of astragalus powder mixed with a little water to the affected areas, 2-3 times a day.

- To **improve digestion**, take astragalus supplements or incorporate astragalus root into soups and broths on a regular basis.

- In case of **respiratory infections,** inhale steam from an astragalus decoction to clear the respiratory tract.

- If you have **trouble sleeping,** drink astragalus tea before bedtime to improve the quality of your sleep.

ASTRAGALUS IN THE KITCHEN

Astragale and Chicken Soup

INGREDIENTS: 1 dried astragalus root, 200 g chicken breast, 1 carrot, 1 onion, 2 liters water, salt and pepper.

1. Cut the chicken, carrot and onion into small pieces.

2. Place all ingredients in a saucepan, including the astragalus root.

3. Cover with 2 liters of water and bring to the boil.

4. Reduce heat and simmer for 1-2 hours.

5. Strain the soup and season to taste with salt and pepper.

6. Serve hot and enjoy this nutritious soup with its many health benefits.

GOJI BERRY
(LYCIUM BARBARUM)

AN ANTIOXIDANT SUPERFRUIT

*Now let's discover a fruit that has earned a reputation
as a superfood in the Western world: the goji berry. Rich
in nutrients, this bright red berry is a health treasure.*

Native to China, where it has been cultivated for over
2,000 years, the goji berry is highly esteemed in traditional
Chinese medicine for its multiple benefits. These berries,
also known as the "fruit of longevity", are credited with
prolonging life and curing many ailments. They contain a
wealth of nutrients, including vitamins, minerals,
antioxidants and amino acids. In ancient China, they were
often used to treat problems such as diabetes, hypertension,
fever and eye disease, as well as to improve immune
function and longevity. With such a variety of nutrients and

health benefits, it's no wonder that goji berry's popularity has exploded worldwide, earning it a prominent place on superfood shelves.

In the kitchen

Goji berries are a versatile ingredient that can be used in a wide range of preparations. **Rich in antioxidants,** it is a valuable addition to morning cereals, yoghurts, fruit salads and even soups and teas. **These antioxidants fight free radicals,** delay skin ageing and strengthen the immune system. **Rich in vitamins and minerals,** they are an invaluable source of essential nutrients that contribute to heart and liver health and help regulate blood sugar levels. Their **high fiber content** also makes them an excellent ally for digestion. These berries go particularly well with ingredients such as dark chocolate, nuts and dried fruit, bringing a sweet touch and pleasant texture to a variety of dishes and snacks. In traditional Chinese medicine, it is used to **boost vitality and energy, improve vision** and **boost immune function**. However, due to their high vitamin A content, they should be eaten in moderation. Adding a few goji berries to your recipes can bring a unique flavor and increase the nutritional value of your dishes, while benefiting from their many beneficial properties.

HEALING WITH GOJI BERRY

- **For vision,** steep a handful of goji berries in hot water and drink this tea regularly to improve eye health thanks to its rich antioxidant content.

- **In case of fatigue or weakness**, consume a handful of dried goji berries daily to revitalize the body and boost energy levels.

- **To boost the immune system**, include goji berries in your diet on a regular basis, as they are rich in vitamins and minerals that stimulate the immune system.

- **To maintain healthy skin**, apply a decoction of goji berries to the skin to benefit from its anti-aging and revitalizing properties.

- **For diabetics,** consume goji berries as part of a balanced diet to help regulate blood sugar levels.

- **If you suffer from high blood pressure,** include goji berries in your diet, as they help maintain healthy blood pressure.

- **To improve digestion,** regularly add goji berries to your meals, as they are rich in fiber.

GOJI BERRY IN THE KITCHEN

Revitalizing goji berry smoothie

INGREDIENTS: 1 banana, 1 cup strawberries, 2 tbsp goji berries, 1 tbsp honey, 1 cup almond milk, 1/2 cup ice cubes.

1. Place goji berries in a bowl of water for about 10 minutes to rehydrate.

2. In a blender, add the banana, strawberries, rehydrated goji berries, honey, almond milk and ice cubes.

3. Blend until smooth and creamy.

4. Serve immediately and enjoy your antioxidant-rich, flavorful smoothie!

RED JUJUBE
(ZIZIPHUS JUJUBA)

A SWEET TREASURE FROM THE FAR EAST

Let's delve into the culinary and medicinal traditions of the Far East and discover red jujube, a tasty and medicinal fruit often overshadowed by more common ingredients.

Red jujube, also known as red date or Chinese date, is a fruit native to China, where it has been cultivated for over 4,000 years. It plays a crucial role in traditional Chinese medicine, recognized for its multiple health benefits. Jujube is prized for its mild flavor and nutritional content, and is used in a variety of culinary preparations and natural remedies throughout Asia and beyond. It has been the object of cults and traditions, being associated with longevity and prosperity. Red jujubes are often eaten dried, resembling dates, but can also be eaten fresh. They are rich in vitamins, minerals and antioxidants and are reputed to improve digestion, sleep and reduce anxiety. This versatile fruit has migrated to other continents, adapting to different climates and soils, enriching the culinary and medicinal diversity of different cultures.

In the kitchen

Red jujube is a versatile fruit that can be easily incorporated into many dishes. It is **richly sweet**, making it an excellent ingredient for desserts such as pies and jams. **Rich in fiber,** it helps **improve digestion** and regulate intestinal transit. Red jujubes are **excellent for cardiovascular health**, thanks to their content of antioxidants and heart-protecting phytochemicals. They can be eaten fresh, dried or used to make teas and decoctions. In Chinese cuisine, they are often used to sweeten soups and porridges, adding a touch of balanced sweetness to savory dishes. **A source of vitamin C,** they boost the immune system and skin health. Red jujube is also used to make syrups and sweet liquids, perfect for flavoring drinks and cocktails. Despite its natural sweetness, red jujube has a **low glycemic index**, making it a healthy sugar for diabetics. It's a precious fruit, bringing not only a delicate, sweet flavor to dishes, but also a host of health benefits, making it a must-have in the daily diet.

HEALING WITH RED JUJUBE

- To combat **insomnia**, make a tea with a few dried red jujubes, a teaspoon of honey and boiling water. Steep for 10 minutes and drink before bed.

- In case of **stress or anxiety,** consume red jujube regularly as a tea or decoction. Add a few jujubes to water and simmer for 20 minutes.

- **For digestive** problems, eat a few dried red jujubes or prepare a decoction with these fruits to soothe the digestive system.

- For **constipation**, red jujube is rich in fiber and can be eaten regularly.

- For **skin inflammation**, apply a poultice of crushed red jujubes mixed with a little water.

- To boost the **immune system**, consume red jujube in various forms, whether fresh, dried, as a tea, or as a decoction.

- If you have **weight problems**, include red jujube in your diet. Its high fiber content and low glycemic index make it an ideal weight-loss ally.

RED JUJUBE IN THE KITCHEN

Red Jujube Tea

INGREDIENTS: 5 to 6 dried red jujubes, 1 cinnamon stick, 1 piece fresh ginger (approx. 2 cm), 1 l water, honey (optional).

1. Rinse the dried red jujubes and place in a saucepan.

2. Add the cinnamon stick and the peeled, sliced piece of fresh ginger.

3. Pour 1 liter of water into the saucepan.

4. Bring to the boil, then reduce heat and simmer for 15-20 minutes.

5. Strain the tea into a mug and add honey to taste if you wish.

6. Enjoy this hot, comforting tea with all its health benefits!

FO-TI
(HE SHOU WU)

ELIXIR OF LONGEVITY AND VITALITY

Discover fo-ti, a precious Chinese herb renowned for its revitalizing and regenerating properties, and an integral part of traditional Chinese medicine.

Fo-ti, also known as he shou wu, is a traditional Chinese medicinal herb. This herb is widely used to prolong longevity, increase vitality and preserve youthfulness. According to legend, a barren man named He Shou Wu lived to the age of 130 after regularly consuming fo-ti, which restored his fertility, strength and hair color. The herb was named in his honor. Fo-ti is a kidney and liver tonic and is said to nourish blood and yin. In traditional Chinese medicine, it is used to treat knee and lumbar weakness, infertility, impotence, chronic constipation in the elderly and chronic liver and kidney disease. Fo-ti is also used in combination with other herbs to treat hair loss and thinning, and to prevent premature graying. It is often combined with revitalizing tonics to strengthen the body and preserve youthfulness.

In the kitchen

Fo-ti is often consumed as a tea or incorporated into soups and stews to benefit from its **revitalizing** and **restorative** properties. It not only has an honorable place in the world of traditional medicine, but is also used as an ingredient in many Asian dishes. It blends well with other herbs and spices, and can add an earthy flavor to a variety of dishes. Its **adaptogenic** nature helps combat **stress** and **fatigue**, and its **antioxidant** properties are particularly sought-after for preventing premature ageing. It is commonly used to concoct tonics and elixirs aimed at **boosting the immune system**, **improving blood circulation** and **balancing energy levels**. People seeking to improve their health naturally can incorporate fo-ti into their diet by adding the dried root to soups, herbal teas or decoctions. Some also use it as a dietary supplement in powder, tincture or capsule form to boost **vitality** and **longevity**. Beware, however, of excessive consumption, which can lead to undesirable effects such as gastrointestinal disorders, and it is advisable to consult a health professional before starting fo-ti supplementation.

HEALING WITH FO-TI

- For **fatigue** and **weakness,** take a teaspoon of dried fo-ti root, add to a cup of water and boil for 10 to 15 minutes. Drink this decoction once a day.

- For **hair loss,** incorporate fo-ti into your diet by taking a teaspoon of fo-ti powder every day.

- To boost the **immune system**, eat dishes containing fo-ti, such as soups and stews, on a regular basis.

- For **constipation**, fo-ti can be taken as a tea, once a day, to help regulate the digestive system.

- In the event of **premature graying,** use fo-ti as a dietary supplement in accordance with the dosage recommended on the packaging.

- To improve **sexual vitality**, consume fo-ti regularly, in powder, tincture or capsule form, as recommended by a health professional.

- If you're looking to **rejuvenate your body and mind**, make fo-ti part of your daily wellness routine.

FO-TI IN THE KITCHEN

Revitalizing Fo-Ti Soup

INGREDIENTS: 1 tablespoon dried fo-ti root, 1 liter water, 200 g shiitake mushrooms, 1 piece fresh ginger (approx. 5 cm), 2 carrots, 1 onion, soy sauce, salt, pepper.

1. Chop the onion and slice the carrots. Grate the ginger.

2. Place the water, onion, carrots, mushrooms, ginger and fo-ti root in a saucepan. Bring to the boil.

3. Reduce the heat and simmer for about 30 minutes.

4. Season with soy sauce, salt and pepper to taste. Then enjoy this soup, which combines the benefits of fo-ti and vegetables for optimum health!

SCHISANDRA

ENERGY AND BALANCE

Discover schisandra, the multi-faceted berry native to China and Russia. Explore its culinary virtues and health benefits, while savoring its unique, complex taste.

Schisandra, also known as wu wei zi in China, is a berry that comes from a climbing vine in the Chinese and Russian regions. This red berry is renowned for its five distinct flavors: sweet, salty, bitter, pungent and acidic, representing the five elements of traditional Chinese medicine. Used for centuries in China and Russia, it is considered one of the 50 fundamental herbs of traditional Chinese medicine. The Chinese have long valued it for its balancing properties and its ability to strengthen vital energy, or qi. Practitioners of traditional Russian medicine have also recognized schisandra for its ability to improve stamina and productivity, while reducing stress. It is known to harmonize and balance body and mind, strengthening resilience to stress and fatigue, and increasing stamina and concentration.

In the kitchen

Schisandra blends well in a variety of dishes and beverages, providing not only complex flavors but also **numerous health benefits**. Used as an **infusion**, it awakens the senses with its multiple flavors and **invigorates the body**. It is also a choice ingredient for **syrups and jams**, adding **energy and balance** to your breakfasts. Schisandra is also used as a **dietary supplement**, often in powder or capsule form, for its **adaptogenic** properties, which help the body **adapt to stress** and **balance its energies**. Its rich **antioxidant** content makes it an ally in the **fight against cell ageing**. It can also be incorporated into sweet recipes, adding a unique touch to desserts. When using it in cooking, it is essential to balance it with other flavors so as not to dominate the dish. Its berries can be infused in hot water with a little honey to make a deliciously invigorating drink, or added to sauces or marinades to enrich meat or vegetable dishes. By incorporating schisandra into your diet, you benefit not only from its remarkable properties, but also from an incomparable taste journey.

TREATMENT WITH SCHISANDRA

- For **fatigue,** take a teaspoon of dried schisandra berries. Infuse in a cup of hot water for 10 minutes. Drink this infusion twice a day.

- When **stressed,** chew a few schisandra berries every day to help reduce stress levels and improve concentration.

- To improve **concentration,** take one teaspoon of schisandra powder in a glass of water or juice once a day.

- For **sleep disorders**, infuse a teaspoon of berries in boiling water and drink before bedtime.

- If you suffer from **liver problems,** consume schisandra tea regularly to support liver function.

- For **energy balance,** mix a teaspoon of schisandra powder with honey and consume it every morning.

- For **aging skin,** apply schisandra oil diluted with carrier oil to the skin to improve skin elasticity and reduce wrinkles.

SCHISANDRA IN THE KITCHEN

Iced Schisandra Tea

INGREDIENTS: 1 tbsp dried schisandra berries, 1 liter water, honey or agave syrup to taste, lemon slices, mint leaves.

1. Bring the water to the boil in a saucepan.

2. Add the dried schisandra berries to the boiling water. - Leave to infuse for 15-20 minutes.

3. Strain the infusion to remove the berries and leave to cool.

4. Add honey or agave syrup to taste and stir well.

5. Serve iced tea with lemon slices and mint leaves.

6. Enjoy this refreshing and soothing drink!

This schisandra iced tea is not only refreshing, it's also a great way to enjoy the many health benefits of this unique berry.

EUCOMMIA
(EUCOMMIA ULMOIDES)

FOR RENEWED VITALITY

Let's discover eucommia, a traditional Chinese medicinal plant. This tree, little known in the West, is nevertheless recognized for its many health benefits.

Native to China, eucommia is renowned for its beneficial effects on bone and joint health. This tree has a long history in traditional Chinese medicine, where it has been used for thousands of years to strengthen the skeleton and muscles. Eucommia leaves are generally used to prepare teas and extracts, which are then consumed for their medicinal properties. The tree's bark is also highly prized for its therapeutic qualities. It is harvested in a sustainable manner to preserve the tree and its environment. Indeed, traditional Chinese medicine attaches great importance to harmony with nature and balance of body and mind.

Eucommia is respected not only for its medicinal attributes, but also for its robustness. Indeed, the tree is capable of surviving and thriving in a wide range of climatic conditions, symbolizing strength and resilience. Eucommia is therefore a symbol of longevity and vitality in Chinese culture.

In the kitchen

Eucommia, particularly its leaves, is often used in cooking as a **revitalizing tea**. As well as being soothing, this tea is known for its **anti-inflammatory** and **antihypertensive properties**. Those seeking to improve **bone and joint health** will find eucommia a valuable ally. The abundant **antioxidants** present in eucommia leaves also help combat cellular aging and strengthen the immune system. Fans of healthy cooking can add a few eucommia leaves to their salads to enjoy its benefits, or even use it in powder form as a dietary supplement. In traditional Chinese medicine, eucommia is often combined with other herbs to balance the effects and enhance the health benefits. It's important to note that, although its benefits are many, eucommia should be consumed in moderation. Excessive consumption could lead to undesirable effects. As always, it is advisable to consult a qualified health professional or herbalist before incorporating new herbs into one's diet, especially in cases of pre-existing medical conditions or when taking medication.

TREATMENT WITH EUCOMMIA

- For **high blood pressure,** infuse a few eucommia leaves in hot water and drink the infusion daily.

- To strengthen **bones and joints**, prepare a decoction of eucommia bark and drink regularly.

- If you suffer from **chronic fatigue,** drink eucommia tea regularly to improve your vitality.

- For **stress,** mix a few eucommia leaves into your smoothies or juices, it can help reduce stress levels.

- **For inflammatory** problems, use eucommia essential oil diluted in a carrier oil, applied topically.

- For **back pain,** infuse eucommia bark in boiling water and drink the decoction once or twice a day.

- If you're looking to **boost your immune system**, include eucommia leaves in your regular diet.

EUCOMMIA IN THE KITCHEN

Eucommia Revitalizing Tea

INGREDIENTS: 1 to 2 tablespoons dried eucommia leaves, 500 ml water, honey or sugar to taste.

1. Bring the water to the boil.

2. Add the dried eucommia leaves.

3. Leave to infuse for 5 to 10 minutes, depending on taste.

4. Strain and sweeten with honey or sugar to taste.

5. Enjoy this revitalizing tea and benefit from the invigorating properties of eucommia.

This tea is not only delicious but also therapeutic, making the consumption of eucommia both pleasurable and beneficial. It's a wonderful way to enjoy the benefits of eucommia while indulging in a soothing beverage.

REISHI
(GANODERMA LUCIDUM)

THE ELIXIR OF LONGEVITY

We're off to the East this time, to discover a "superfood" revered in Asian cultures: reishi or "mushroom of immortality", a precious dietary and medicinal supplement.

Reishi, also known as lingzhi in China, is a mushroom that has been used for over 2,000 years in traditional Asian medicine, particularly in China and Japan. It was renowned for its unique medicinal properties and its ability to promote longevity and health. This highly prized mushroom was once reserved for emperors and royalty. It was said to regenerate vital energy and harmonize mind, body and soul. Reishi is known for its distinctive appearance, with a bright red cap and glazed texture. It grows on tree stumps and roots, mainly on plum trees. In ancient times, its rarity contributed to its treasure status, but today, thanks to modern cultivation, it has become widely available.

In the kitchen

Reishi is a spice that not only has a place in traditional medicine, but can also add a rich, earthy flavor to a variety of dishes. Reishi's **adaptogenic properties** make it an excellent addition to herbal teas and soups, helping the body to resist stress of all kinds. It can be found as a powder or dried slices and added to hot drinks or dishes to benefit from its **antioxidant**, **anti-inflammatory** and **immunomodulating** properties. It's worth noting, however, that its distinct taste can be strong, so it's advisable to start with small quantities and adjust according to preference. Reishi has the ability to **boost the immune system**, **improve mental health** and **reduce inflammation** and **oxidative stress** in the body. Incorporating this mushroom into the diet can therefore offer a range of health benefits, as well as adding a unique touch to your culinary preparations. However, its culinary use is not as widespread as its medicinal uses due to its bitter taste, but this in no way reduces its benefits when used as a dietary supplement.

TREATMENT WITH REISHI

- For **immunity and stress**, make reishi tea by infusing dried reishi slices in hot water for 30 minutes. Drink one cup a day.

- For **sleep problems,** mix a teaspoon of reishi powder in a cup of hot milk before bedtime.

- For **chronic fatigue,** take reishi supplements according to package instructions.

- To combat **inflammation**, regularly add reishi to your diet in tea or supplement form.

- To **improve liver function,** use reishi in supplement form or as a powder added to your meals or drinks.

- If you have **skin problems,** apply a cream containing reishi.

- For **high blood pressure,** include reishi in your diet on a regular basis, either as a tea or a supplement.

REISHI IN THE KITCHEN

Revitalizing Reishi Soup

INGREDIENTS: 5 dried reishi slices, 1.5 L water, 2 chopped carrots, 2 celery stalks, 1 chopped onion, 2 minced garlic cloves, 1 tbsp soy sauce, salt and pepper to taste.

1. Bring the water to the boil and add the dried reishi slices. Reduce heat and simmer for 1 hour.

2. Remove the reishi from the water and add the carrots, celery, onion and garlic. Simmer until vegetables are tender.

3. Add soy sauce, salt and pepper. Adjust seasoning to taste.

4. Serve hot and enjoy the revitalizing benefits of this nutrient-rich soup.

CORDYCEPS
(CORDYCEPS SINENSIS)

ENERGY AND VITALITY

Accrues Now let's discover a fascinating "spice" that's not really a spice in the traditional sense: cordyceps, a mushroom prized in traditional Chinese and Tibetan medicine.

Cordyceps, sometimes called "caterpillar fungus", is a genus of parasitic fungi mainly found in the mountainous regions of China, Nepal and Tibet. It has a rich and ancient history as a medicinal remedy. Ancient Chinese emperors valued it for its vitality- and energy-boosting properties, and it was often reserved for kings and nobility. Cordyceps is renowned for its health benefits, which include increasing stamina, reducing fatigue and improving kidney and lung function. Its anti-aging and aphrodisiac properties are also valued in traditional medicine. It is an adaptogen, helping the body to adapt to stress and restore balance.

In the kitchen

Cordyceps is not commonly used in cooking like ajowan, but rather consumed in supplement or powder form. However, its **energy-boosting effect** and ability to **improve stamina** make it particularly beneficial for those seeking to optimize their physical and mental performance. Athletes, in particular, can benefit from consuming cordyceps to **improve endurance and reduce fatigue**. Traditionally, it is often prepared as a decoction or infused in hot water to make tea. The taste of cordyceps is earthy and mild, blending well with other medicinal herbs or teas. It is **rich in antioxidants**, making it useful for combating oxidative stress and inflammation in the body. In addition, it is recognized for its **adaptogenic** properties, which help the body adapt to stress, restoring balance and strengthening the immune system. Traditional medicine also recommends it for **improving kidney and lung function**, and it is often used by those seeking to optimize the health of these vital organs.

CURE YOURSELF WITH CORDYCEPS

- To **improve physical performance**, mix a teaspoon of cordyceps powder with your morning smoothie or juice. Consume this preparation before your workouts.

- For **fatigue and stress**, prepare a tea by infusing a teaspoon of cordyceps in hot water for 5-10 minutes. Drink this tea once or twice a day.

- For **lung problems** and to **boost the immune system**, regularly include cordyceps in your diet, in supplement or powder form, as recommended by your doctor or healthcare professional.

- If you suffer from **sleep disorders or insomnia**, take cordyceps supplements or infusions regularly.

- For **libido problems,** take cordyceps in supplement form, after consulting a health professional.

- To **improve kidney function**, include cordyceps in your diet on a regular basis, in powder or supplement form.

CORDYCEPS IN THE KITCHEN

Cordyceps revitalizing tea

INGREDIENTS: 1 teaspoon cordyceps powder, 1 cup boiling water, 1 teaspoon honey (optional), 1 lemon slice (optional).

1. Place cordyceps powder in a cup.

2. Pour boiling water over the cordyceps.

3. Leave to infuse for 5-10 minutes.

4. Add honey and lemon if desired, to enhance flavour.

5. Stir well and enjoy this revitalizing tea.

In addition to its unique taste, this drink will give you energy and vitality, while boosting your immune system and improving your respiratory and kidney functions.

DANG GUI
(ANGELICA SINENSIS)

FOR FEMININE HARMONY

Let's discover dang mistletoe, a spice revered in traditional Chinese medicine, also known as Chinese angelica, reputed for its many benefits, including balancing feminine energies.

Dang mistletoe, or Chinese angelica, is a major medicinal plant in Chinese tradition. Cultivated mainly in China, Korea and Japan, dang gui is often called the "female ginseng" for its beneficial properties for women's health. Used for thousands of years in traditional Chinese medicine, dang gui is reputed to promote blood circulation and harmonize the female reproductive system. It is often used to relieve symptoms of premenstrual syndrome and menopause, and to tone the blood. The roots of dang gui are rich in phytochemicals, including coumarins, phytosterols and polysaccharides, which give the plant its diverse medicinal properties. The Chinese also use dang gui in cooking, often to create nutritious soups and broths, combining health benefits with gustatory pleasures.

In the kitchen

In addition to its medicinal benefits, **dang mistletoe is also an** ingredient of **Asian cuisine**. It is mainly used in **soups and broths**, enriching dishes with its unique flavors and beneficial properties. **Rich in nutrients** and beneficial components, it transforms every dish into a revitalizing culinary experience. Its **harmonizing and invigorating** properties make it an ingredient of choice for improving general well-being, and it is particularly appreciated by women for its balancing effects. Incorporating dang mistletoe into the daily diet can **promote blood circulation**, **balance feminine energies**, and provide a feeling of well-being and vitality. However, its use must be moderate and balanced, as excessive consumption can have undesirable effects. With its wealth of active ingredients and its ability to transform dishes, dang gui is a treasure trove of traditional Asian cuisine and medicine, enabling everyone to explore new flavors while enjoying its many health benefits.

HEALING WITH DANG GUI

- To **regulate menstruation**, take a tablespoon of dried dang mistletoe root. Boil it in 2 cups of water until the water has reduced by half. Drink this decoction once a day.

- For **menopausal symptoms,** mix a teaspoon of dang mistletoe powder with honey and consume twice a day.

- To relieve **abdominal pain**, crush dang mistletoe root and infuse in hot water. Drink as a tea on a regular basis.

- For **anemia,** combine dang mistletoe with iron-rich herbs such as nettle and red clover and take as a herbal tea.

- If you suffer from **chronic fatigue,** take dang mistletoe regularly as a decoction to improve your energy levels.

- For **dyspepsia,** drink a decoction of dang mistletoe after meals to aid digestion.

- For **dry skin or eczema**, apply dang mistletoe oil mixed with a carrier oil to the affected areas.

DANG GUI IN THE KITCHEN

Revitalizing Dang Gui Soup

INGREDIENTS: 15 g dang mistletoe root, 150 g chicken, 2 carrots, 1 turnip, 1 onion, 1.5 L water, salt and pepper.

1. Wash, peel and chop the vegetables. Cut chicken into pieces.

2. Put the vegetables, chicken and dang mistletoe root in a saucepan.

3. Add 1.5 L of water and bring to the boil.

4. Reduce heat and simmer for 1 to 1? hours.

5. Season with salt and pepper to taste.

6. Serve hot, and enjoy this nutritious, comforting soup!

7.

PART III: OTHER POPULAR MEDICINAL PLANTS

These popular medicinal plants are often available in a variety of forms. Careful research and selection of reliable, environmentally-friendly sources are essential to obtaining high-quality products.

MINT
(MENTHA)

FOR A TOUCH OF FRESHNESS AND WELL-BEING

Let's dive into the fragrant world of mint, a prized aromatic plant that brightens our gardens and enriches our dishes with its characteristic freshness and beneficial properties.

Native to Europe and the Middle East, mint has been known since Antiquity. The Romans and Greeks used it to perfume their baths and drinks, as well as in their medicinal preparations. The Egyptians appreciated mint for its digestive properties and as a preservative. Mint has spread throughout the world, becoming an indispensable ingredient in various cuisines and medicinal traditions. It is known for its refreshing fragrance and pungent, fresh taste. In addition to its culinary uses, mint is also renowned for its medicinal properties, notably its soothing effects on the

116

digestive system and its cooling and analgesic powers. Mint leaves contain phytochemicals, such as menthol, which are responsible for its healing properties and distinctive aroma. There are many varieties of mint, including peppermint, spearmint and watermint, each with its own specific characteristics and uses.

In the kitchen

Mint is a culinary treasure. **Versatile and refreshing,** it enhances salads, desserts and drinks. Mint's penetrating taste makes it an ideal ingredient for enhancing flavors, whether used fresh, dried or as an essential oil. Its **digestive properties** make it a must-have in many cultures, especially for concocting soothing teas after meals. Whether in Lebanese tabbouleh, Moroccan mint tea or Greek yoghurt sauces, mint infuses dishes with its freshness and distinctive aroma. Its **antispasmodic and anti-inflammatory properties** make it an ally in soothing headaches and muscular pains, often in essential oil or infusion form. But mint is not only appreciated for its medicinal and culinary virtues, it is also an asset to **oral health** thanks to its refreshing and antiseptic effect, hence its frequent presence in toothpastes and mouthwashes. Ultimately, mint is a versatile herb that combines flavor, freshness and health benefits, making our culinary experiences even more enjoyable and healthy.

HEALING WITH MINT

- To soothe **headaches,** infuse a few fresh mint leaves in boiling water and drink the resulting herbal tea.

- For **difficult digestion**, prepare an infusion of mint. Steep for 10 minutes and drink after meals.

- To relieve **itchy skin,** apply crushed mint leaves directly to the skin.

- If you have **respiratory problems,** inhale the vapors of a mint decoction to clear the airways.

- For **muscular pain**, use a few drops of mint essential oil mixed with a carrier oil and massage into the affected area.

- To treat **mouth infections,** rinse your mouth with a cooled mint infusion.

- For **acne,** apply mint essential oil diluted in carrier oil to purify the skin.

- To keep **insects** away, diffuse mint essential oil in your environment.

MINT IN THE KITCHEN

Mint Tabbouleh

INGREDIENTS: 200 g bulgur, 3 tomatoes, 1 cucumber, 1 bunch fresh mint, 1 bunch flat-leaf parsley, 1 lemon, 3 tbsp olive oil, salt.

1. Place the bulgur in a bowl and cover with boiling water. Leave to swell for 30 minutes, then drain.

2. Dice the tomatoes and cucumber.

3. Finely chop the mint and parsley.

4. Mix the bulgur, vegetables, mint and parsley in a salad bowl.

5. Drizzle with lemon juice and olive oil. Add salt to taste.

6. Mix well and refrigerate for at least an hour before serving. Enjoy your meal!

LEMON BALM
(MELISSA OFFICINALIS)

A SOOTHING REMEDY

Let's discover lemon balm, an aromatic plant much appreciated both for its medicinal virtues and for its sweet, refreshing lemony aroma, which appeals to palates the world over.

Lemon balm, also known as citronella or lemon grass, is native to southern Europe and the Mediterranean region. It has been known since antiquity, and was highly prized by the Greeks and Romans for its medicinal properties. The name "melissa" comes from the Greek "melissa" meaning "bee", due to its sweet aroma which attracts these insects. Historically, this plant was dedicated to the goddess of hunting, Diana, and was used to treat scorpion bites and insect stings. In the Middle Ages, lemon balm was cultivated in monastery gardens for its soothing and digestive virtues. It was a key ingredient in the Elixir of Long Life, a popular alchemical remedy. Lemon balm continues to be used to relieve a variety of ailments, including digestive disorders, headaches and nervous tension.

In the kitchen

Lemon balm is often used to **flavor** various dishes and beverages, thanks to its lemony flavor. It goes particularly well with seafood, salads and desserts, adding a note of **freshness**. It is ideal for **flavoring** oils and vinegars, giving a **unique flavor** and **pleasant aroma**. In herbal tea, lemon balm is recognized for its **soothing** and **digestive** properties, helping to relax the nervous system and improve digestion. It is also rich in **antioxidants**, beneficial for overall health and well-being. Lemon balm leaves can also be used to make **syrups**, **liqueurs**, jams and sorbets. Be careful, however, to use it in moderation, as its distinctive taste can become overpowering. Use it fresh for optimum aroma, or dried, but in smaller quantities so as not to overshadow the other flavors in the dish. Lemon balm is a versatile herb which, while adding a touch of freshness and a lemony fragrance, enriches the palette of tastes in cooking while offering numerous health benefits.

TAKING CARE OF YOURSELF WITH LEMON BALM

- To soothe **nervousness** and **insomnia**, infuse a tablespoon of lemon balm leaves in a cup of boiling water for 10 minutes. Drink before bedtime.

- For **digestive problems**, prepare a decoction by placing a few lemon balm leaves in boiling water. Leave to infuse and drink after meals.

- For **headaches** and **migraines**, massage your temples with a few drops of lemon balm essential oil diluted in a carrier oil.

- To relieve **insect bites,** apply a few crushed fresh lemon balm leaves directly to the bite.

- If you suffer from **herpes or fever blisters**, apply one drop of lemon balm essential oil diluted in a vegetable oil several times a day.

- For **mouth infections,** use cooled lemon balm infusion as a mouthwash to soothe inflammation and irritation.

- In case of **nervous tension or stress,** inhale the aroma of lemon balm essential oil several times a day.

LEMON BALM IN THE KITCHEN

Lemon balm sorbet

INGREDIENTS: 1 cup sugar, 2 cups water, 1 cup fresh lemon balm leaves, juice of 2 lemons.

1. Bring the water and sugar to the boil in a saucepan until the sugar has dissolved.

2. Remove from the heat, add the lemon balm leaves and leave to infuse for around 30 minutes.

3. Strain the mixture and add the lemon juice.

4. Leave to cool completely, then pour into an ice-cream maker.

5. Set the sorbet according to your machine's instructions.

6. Once the sorbet has set, serve garnished with lemon balm leaves. Enjoy this refreshingly fragrant dessert!

CHAMOMILE
(MATRICARIA CHAMOMILLA)

NATURAL SOOTHING

Let's immerse ourselves in the gentle, comforting world of chamomile, a plant with multiple virtues, renowned for its soothing and healing properties, and frequently used in different cultures around the world.

Chamomile, an ancestral medicinal plant, inevitably evokes relaxation. Known since ancient Egypt, it was dedicated to the sun for its curative properties against fever. The Greeks, for their part, used it for its anti-inflammatory virtues and gave it its name, "kamaimelon", meaning "apple of the soil" due to the apple-like scent of its flowers. During the Middle Ages, this plant was one of the main ingredients in potions and remedies to treat various afflictions. In Victorian times, it was often consumed in herbal tea form for its soothing effect and delicious aroma. Chamomile is a versatile plant, growing throughout Europe, Asia and North Africa. It is prized not only for its pleasant aroma and medicinal properties, but also for its culinary and cosmetic applications. Chamomile is renowned for its anti-inflammatory, antispasmodic and calming properties. It is widely used to soothe digestive disorders, skin inflammation, menstrual pain and nervous tension.

In the kitchen

Chamomile is best known as a relaxing herbal tea, but its culinary uses don't stop there. **Soothing and digestive,** it can be incorporated into many dishes and pastries to give them a floral touch and a delicate aroma. Chamomile flowers can be used fresh or dried, and are an excellent addition to salads, desserts, and even some main courses, adding a soft, sweet note. Chefs also use chamomile to infuse creams and milks used in creamy desserts and ice creams, imparting a subtle, sophisticated flavor. **Digestive and anti-inflammatory,** chamomile is a healthy condiment that enhances the **flavor** and **nutritional benefits** of dishes. It is an excellent way of incorporating **soothing properties** into the daily diet. Finally, chamomile can be added to a variety of drinks such as smoothies and cocktails for an original, fragrant twist. It is essential, however, to use it sparingly, as its distinctive taste can overpower other flavors in the dish.

HEALING WITH CHAMOMILE

- **For insomnia,** infuse 1 to 2 teaspoons of chamomile flowers in a cup of hot water for 10 minutes. Drink this tea before going to bed.

125

- **For digestive problems**, prepare an herbal tea with a tablespoon of chamomile flowers in a cup of boiling water. Leave to infuse for 10 minutes and drink after meals.

- **For skin irritations or slight burns**, apply chamomile compresses. Infuse a few chamomile flowers in water, soak a clean piece of cloth and apply to the affected area.

- **If your mouth is inflamed,** use an infusion of chamomile as a mouthwash, after letting it cool.

- **To relieve menstrual cramps,** drink several cups of chamomile tea throughout the day.

- **For anxiety or stress,** drink chamomile tea regularly throughout the day.

- **For eye problems such as conjunctivitis,** use cooled chamomile compresses on your closed eyes.

CHAMOMILE IN THE KITCHEN

Chamomile and lemon cake

INGREDIENTS: 200 g flour, 150 g sugar, 125 g butter, 4 eggs, zest and juice of one lemon, 2 tbsp dried chamomile flowers, 1 sachet baking powder.

1. Preheat oven to 180°C.

2. In a bowl, mix butter and sugar until creamy.

3. Add the eggs one at a time, mixing well between each addition.

4. Add the lemon zest and juice, then the chamomile flowers.

5. Mix the flour and baking powder, then stir into the mixture.

6. Pour the batter into a buttered and floured mould.

7. Bake for about 35 minutes or until a knife comes out clean.

8. Leave to cool before unmoulding, then enjoy!

ALOE VERA
(ALOE BARBADENSIS MILLER)

SOVEREIGN OF THE DESERT

Let's dive into the mysterious and invigorating world of Aloe Vera, a "thorny" plant that hides its secrets, revealing a treasure trove of benefits for our health and our palate.

Aloe Vera, also known as "Lily of the Desert", is a succulent plant belonging to the Liliaceae family. Its history goes back more than 6,000 years; the ancient Egyptians called it the "plant of immortality" and used it to treat a variety of ailments. It conquered various civilizations, including the Greeks, Romans and Indians, for its medicinal properties and its ability to treat a multitude of ailments, from constipation to skin burns. This plant has the ability to survive in arid environments, thanks to its fleshy, water-retaining leaves. These leaves contain the precious Aloe Vera gel, rich in vitamins, minerals, amino acids and enzymes. Aloe Vera's popularity has spanned the ages and continents, and today it is recognized worldwide for its moisturizing, soothing and healing properties, while also gaining notoriety in the culinary world.

In the kitchen

Aloe Vera is not only an elixir of well-being, it's also a **versatile ingredient** in the kitchen. Fresh Aloe Vera segments can be **incorporated into smoothies, juices, or even salads**, for a nutritious boost. Aloe Vera's subtle, slightly bitter taste balances perfectly with sweet and tart flavors, making it suitable for **refreshing desserts** or energy drinks. **Rich in antioxidants, vitamins A and C, and digestive enzymes**, Aloe Vera is a superb addition for those seeking to adopt a healthy, balanced diet. It also **aids digestion and improves hydration, making it** a valuable ally in maintaining optimal health. However, care should be taken with its use, as consumed in large quantities, it can have a laxative effect. It is therefore advisable to consume it in moderation, and to be attentive to individual reactions. Aloe Vera's beneficial properties and nutritional profile make it an ingredient worth exploring, both for its taste qualities and for its positive impact on our well-being.

TREATMENT WITH ALOE VERA

- For **burns or skin irritations**, apply pure Aloe Vera gel directly to the affected area. It provides immediate relief and helps the skin heal.

- For **constipation,** consume Aloe Vera juice. Start by taking a small amount and gradually increase the dose, as it can have a laxative effect.

- For **skin hydration,** apply Aloe Vera gel to your face and body. It's excellent for keeping skin hydrated and supple.

- If you have **digestive problems,** drink Aloe Vera juice regularly. It helps soothe and cleanse the digestive system.

- For **mouth ulcers,** apply Aloe Vera gel directly to the affected area several times a day.

- For **acne,** apply Aloe Vera gel to the affected areas to reduce inflammation and infection.

- **For gastroesophageal reflux** disease, drink Aloe Vera juice 20 minutes before meals to reduce inflammation and acid production.

ALOE VERA IN THE KITCHEN

Aloe Vera Smoothie

INGREDIENTS: 1 cup Aloe Vera gel, 1 cup fresh orange juice, 1 ripe banana, 1 tablespoon honey, ice cubes.

1. Blend all ingredients in a blender until smooth and homogeneous.

2. Add ice cubes to taste and blend again.

3. Serve immediately in a tall glass and enjoy this refreshing and beneficial smoothie.

EUCALYPTUS
(EUCALYPTUS GLOBULUS)

FOR A HEALTHY RESPIRATORY SYSTEM

Let's discover eucalyptus, a plant known for its powerful essential oil and penetrating scent, native to Australia and widely used for its medicinal properties.

Eucalyptus is synonymous with the essence of wild Australia. Its name derives from the Greek "eu", meaning good, and "kalypto", to cover, referring to the operculum that covers the flower. It is a plant that has been widely adopted and cultivated throughout the world, notably for its medicinal and antiseptic properties. Australian aborigines have used eucalyptus leaves for centuries to heal wounds and prevent infection. In colonial times, convicts used eucalyptus' antiseptic properties to treat typhoid fever and dysentery. In 1788, the surgeon general of the fleet, who accompanied the first settlers to Australia, praised eucalyptus' properties for treating patients. This aromatic plant is now known and used worldwide to clear the respiratory tract, relieve sore throats and as a natural disinfectant. Eucalyptus essential oil is particularly prized for its multiple therapeutic benefits, including as an anti-inflammatory, antispasmodic, antiseptic and decongestant.

In the kitchen

Thanks to **its distinctive fragrance,** eucalyptus can add a unique touch to a variety of dishes. Although not a spice traditionally used in cooking, its refreshing aroma and minty flavor can enrich both sweet and savory dishes. Eucalyptus leaves are sometimes used to infuse syrups, which can then be added to cocktails, sorbets or pastries. **Its antiseptic and anti-inflammatory properties** also make eucalyptus beneficial in herbal teas for relieving a variety of ailments, such as respiratory infections and throat inflammation. Eucalyptus is a spice **with detoxifying and purifying properties**, making it ideal for making health drinks. Eucalyptus can be blended with other herbs and spices, such as thyme, rosemary or mint, to create therapeutic and tasty blends, perfect to round off a meal. However, it's important to note that eucalyptus should be used sparingly in cooking due to its potency, and some people may be sensitive or allergic to this plant, so a cautious approach is recommended.

TREATMENT WITH EUCALYPTUS

- For **nasal congestion,** pour a few drops of eucalyptus essential oil into hot water and inhale the steam.

- To **soothe a sore throat**, add a teaspoon of dried eucalyptus leaves to a cup of hot water and steep for 10 minutes. Drink this tea up to three times a day.

- If you have **cuts or wounds,** apply a few drops of eucalyptus essential oil diluted in a carrier oil to the affected area for its antiseptic properties.

- For **muscular pain,** mix a few drops of eucalyptus essential oil with a carrier oil and massage the painful area.

- For **respiratory infections,** inhale steam from boiling water mixed with a few drops of eucalyptus essential oil, or drink eucalyptus leaf tea.

- To **fight acne,** mix a drop of eucalyptus essential oil with a teaspoon of coconut oil and apply to affected areas.

- If you have **insect bites,** apply a few drops of eucalyptus essential oil directly to the stung area to relieve the itch.

EUCALYPTUS IN THE KITCHEN

Eucalyptus sorbet

INGREDIENTS: 500 ml water, 200 g sugar, 1 tbsp dried eucalyptus leaves, 2 tbsp lemon juice.

1. Bring the water to the boil and add the dried eucalyptus leaves. Leave to infuse for 10 minutes.

2. Strain the mixture to remove the leaves and return the liquid to the pan.

3. Add the sugar and stir until completely dissolved. Let the syrup cool, then add the lemon juice.

4. Chill the mixture in the refrigerator until well chilled.

5. Pour the mixture into an ice-cream maker and follow the manufacturer's instructions to make the sorbet.

6. Once finished, serve the fresh eucalyptus sorbet and enjoy!

LAVANDER
(LAVANDULA ANGUSTIFOLIA)

FOR TOTAL RELAXATION

Let's begin this new chapter in our world tour of spices and aromatic plants with lavender, a staple of Mediterranean flora, renowned for its relaxing properties and bewitching fragrance.

Native to the Mediterranean basin, lavender is an aromatic plant that is an integral part of Provencal culture. From ancient times to the present day, lavender has been prized for its delicate fragrance and numerous therapeutic virtues. The Romans used it to perfume their baths, linens and interiors, and the Egyptians made it an essential component in the manufacture of perfumes and ointments. In the Middle Ages, it was cultivated in monastery gardens for its medicinal properties and was considered a remedy against the plague. It was not until the 17th century that lavender cultivation became an economic activity in its own right in Provence. Today, lavender is grown all over the world, and its uses are as diverse as they are varied, notably in aromatherapy, perfumery, cooking and skincare products. Lavender is often associated with relaxation, and its essential oil is used to soothe both mind and body.

In the kitchen

Lavender is a versatile plant that can enhance many dishes and beverages. It goes particularly well with honey, citrus and red fruits. **Antiseptic** and **anti-inflammatory**, it can be used to infuse tea, or to flavor cookies, ice creams and savory dishes. Chefs appreciate its ability to enhance flavors and add a floral touch to their creations. Dried lavender flowers can be ground and added to spice blends, or used on their own to perfume sauces, meats or desserts. But lavender isn't just delicious, it's also good for your health. Rich in **antioxidants**, it helps protect the body against free radicals. And thanks to its **digestive properties**, it helps soothe gastrointestinal complaints such as bloating and cramps. Lavender is also said to have **relaxing and soothing** benefits, making it an ingredient of choice for a serene conclusion to a meal. Lavender in cooking should be used in moderation, as its powerful taste can overpower other flavors. It's a natural treasure that deserves its place in our kitchens and gardens.

HEALING WITH LAVENDER

- To soothe **headaches** and **stress**, make an infusion with 1 tablespoon dried lavender flowers to 1 cup boiling water. Leave to infuse for 10 minutes, then strain.

- For **light burns and insect bites**, apply a few drops of lavender essential oil diluted in a vegetable oil to the affected area.

- To help with **insomnia,** put a few drops of lavender essential oil on your pillow or add it to an essential oil diffuser before going to bed.

- For **muscular tension**, prepare a relaxing bath by adding 10 drops of lavender essential oil to the bath water.

- For **skin infections**, apply a drop of lavender essential oil to the wound after cleansing.

- For **digestive problems** such as bloating and cramps, drink lavender tea after meals.

- For **acne-prone skin,** mix a few drops of lavender essential oil into your night cream to help clarify the skin.

LAVENDER IN THE KITCHEN

Lavender cookies

INGREDIENTS: 200 g flour, 100 g butter, 100 g sugar, 1 egg, 1 tbsp dried lavender flowers, 1 tsp baking powder, pinch of salt.

1. Preheat oven to 180°C.

2. Mix the sugar and butter until creamy. Add the egg and mix well.

3. Sift flour, baking powder and salt into the mixture.

4. Add the lavender flowers and mix gently.

5. On a floured surface, roll out the dough to 5 mm thickness and cut out the cookies using a cookie cutter.

6. Place the cookies on a parchment-lined baking sheet and bake for 12-15 minutes, or until golden.

7. Cool on a wire rack before serving.

ARNICA
(ARNICA MONTANA)

A MARVEL FOR THE MUSCLES

Let's discover another remarkable medicinal plant, arnica, known for its anti-inflammatory and healing properties, this time traveling to the mountains of Europe and North America.

Arnica, often considered one of the most effective medicinal plants for healing, has its origins in mountainous regions. Used for centuries, arnica was already known to the Greeks and Romans, who used it to treat a variety of ailments such as bruises and sprains. This perennial plant, which prefers the acidic, siliceous soils of mountain meadows, is mainly used in homeopathic medicine and phytotherapy to treat inflammation, muscular pain and bruising. Arnica flowers are particularly rich in active compounds such as flavonoids, essential oils and sesquiterpene lactones, which give it its unique medicinal properties. Despite its diverse medicinal uses, arnica is not consumed as food due to its toxicity when ingested, and is mainly used in topical or homeopathic form.

In the kitchen

Arnica is not used in cooking because of its **toxicity** when ingested. Indeed, consuming arnica can cause **serious health effects**, such as severe vomiting, muscle weakness and heart irregularities. It is therefore **essential to use arnica only externally**, in the form of ointments, gels, oils, or in homeopathy, where it is very diluted. However, in alternative medicine, it is a **powerful anti-inflammatory and analgesic**, making it ideal for treating **bruises, sprains, muscle aches and skin inflammations**. Arnica extracts are renowned for **soothing sore muscles** and accelerating the healing of bruises. Arnica ointments and oils are widely used by athletes and people suffering from muscle or joint pain. Although arnica cannot be used in cooking or ingested, its role in the world of natural medicine is undeniable, offering **rapid relief** to people suffering from a variety of aches and pains. Careful, informed use of arnica allows you to benefit from its therapeutic properties without risking adverse effects.

TREATMENT WITH ARNICA

- For **muscle pain,** apply an arnica-based ointment to the affected area. Avoid open wounds or cuts, as arnica is toxic when ingested.

- For **sprains or bruises**, use arnica in gel or cream form to reduce inflammation and pain.

- If you have **bruises,** apply arnica oil to the affected area to speed up healing.

- For **skin inflammation,** topical application of arnica cream can help reduce inflammation and relieve pain.

- For **headaches or tension**, try a light massage with arnica oil on the temples, avoiding contact with the eyes.

- For **insect bites,** applying an arnica cream or gel can help reduce pain, swelling and itching.

- For **arthritic pain,** arnica can be used in ointment or gel form to relieve pain and inflammation.

ARNICA IN THE KITCHEN

Arnica is not used in cooking due to its toxicity when ingested. However, here is an example of a recipe for an infusion of arnica for external use:

Arnica infusion for compresses

INGREDIENTS: 2 tbsp dried arnica flowers, 500 ml water.

1. Place the arnica flowers in a container.

2. Bring the water to the boil and pour over the arnica flowers.

3. Leave to infuse for about 15 minutes, then strain.

4. Soak a compress in the cooled infusion and apply to the affected area to relieve muscle pain and bruising. Please note: this infusion is for external use only and must not be ingested!

NETTLE
(URTICA DIOICA)

FOR BENEFITS THAT STING

Let's discover a local plant, nettle, known for its little stings, but overflowing with a multitude of benefits and finding its place as much in our gardens as in our kitchens and pharmacies.

Recognized by its small, stinging needles, nettle is found almost everywhere in the world. This hardy plant has long been overlooked as a weed, but its history goes back to antiquity. The Romans used nettle to stimulate blood circulation by flogging it on the skin. It was also a key ingredient in medieval pharmacopoeia to treat a variety of ailments, including joint pain and kidney disorders. It is a plant rich in minerals, vitamins, proteins and chlorophyll.

It has stood the test of time, remaining a constant in both traditional and modern remedy recipes. Today, nettle is increasingly recognized for its many benefits, gaining new appreciation as a nutritious medicinal and food plant. Scientists are studying its anti-inflammatory and analgesic properties, and its positive effects on urinary and renal health.

In the kitchen

Nettle is a **protein- and nutrient-rich** ingredient, making it an excellent addition to many dishes. Its richness in **iron, calcium and vitamins A and C** makes nettle a plant with **revitalizing** and **strengthening properties**. It is particularly beneficial for people suffering from anemia. Young nettle shoots can be used in soups, pestos or smoothies. Its taste, similar to that of spinach, makes it easy to incorporate into a variety of recipes. In addition to its culinary uses, nettle is also renowned for its **detoxifying and anti-inflammatory properties**. It helps eliminate toxins from the body, supports kidney function and can help relieve joint pain. Nettle is also a **blood tonic**, helping to purify the blood and combat anemia. Be careful, however, to cook it thoroughly to deactivate its stinging hairs! Regular use of nettle in your diet can therefore promote good health and prevent various ailments. If you're looking for new flavours and health benefits, don't hesitate to incorporate nettle into your dishes!

HEALING WITH NETTLE

- **For allergies and inflammation**, make an herbal tea by infusing 1-2 tablespoons of dried

145

nettle leaves in a cup of hot water. Drink up to three cups a day.

- **In case of anemia,** consume iron-rich nettle soup regularly to boost iron levels and improve red blood cell production.

- **For joint pain,** use nettle externally, in the form of a poultice or nettle oil, to benefit from its anti-inflammatory properties.

- **In case of fatigue**, consume nettle juice as a tonic, as it is rich in vitamins and minerals.

- **For skin problems such as acne**, apply nettle oil locally, which has antibacterial and anti-inflammatory properties.

- **For healthy hair,** use nettle water as a rinse after shampooing to strengthen roots and combat dandruff.

- **For water retention or urinary tract infections**, drink nettle tea, which is diuretic and helps eliminate toxins.

NETTLE IN THE KITCHEN

Revitalizing nettle soup

INGREDIENTS: 300 g young nettle shoots, 1 onion, 1 potato, 1 L water, 2 tbsp crème fraîche, salt and pepper.

1. Carefully clean the nettles and chop the onion and potato.

2. Sauté the onion in a little oil until translucent.

3. Add the nettles and potato, and sauté for a few minutes.

4. Add the water, salt and pepper, then simmer for around 20 minutes until the vegetables are tender.

5. Blend the soup until smooth and add the crème fraîche.

6. Adjust seasoning if necessary and serve hot. This revitalizing soup is delicious served with garlic croutons.

CALENDULA
(CALENDULA OFFICINALIS)

GARDEN CARE

Calendula, more commonly known as marigold, is a wonder of nature. Appreciated as much for its beauty as for its therapeutic properties, it is a treasure in gardens and kitchens alike.

Native to southern Europe and western Asia, calendula has a long history of use as a medicinal plant. In the Middle Ages, it was used for its anti-inflammatory and healing properties, and to treat a variety of skin diseases. In traditional medicine, it is often used for its soothing and regenerative properties on the skin, and is a well-known remedy for wounds, burns, eczema and cuts. In addition, calendula flowers have been used as a remedy for sore throats, gastric ulcers and irregular menstruation. Calendula has also been used in cooking, its colorful flowers being used as a substitute for saffron to color and flavor dishes, as well as to decorate salads and other culinary preparations.

In the kitchen

Calendula is used not only to beautify gardens, but also to enhance the taste of various dishes. Its petals have a slightly bitter, spicy taste and are **rich in antioxidants, flavonoids and carotenoids**, giving them **anti-inflammatory and antiviral** properties. They can be used to color rice, pasta and cakes, giving them a lovely golden hue and delicate flavor. In addition to these culinary uses, calendula flowers can be infused in oils to create flavored vinaigrettes, full of **health-boosting properties**. Dried calendula petals can also be added to herbal teas, providing a **soothing drink** for the digestive system and beneficial for the skin. But be warned: although calendula is generally considered safe, it is always advisable to consume in moderation, especially for people allergic to plants in the Asteraceae family, such as chrysanthemum, daisy or arnica. Pregnant or breast-feeding women are advised to seek medical advice before use. Calendula, with its vibrant petals and multiple benefits, is a valuable addition to the kitchen and natural pharmacopoeia, a true treasure of nature.

TAKING CARE OF YOURSELF WITH CALENDULA

- For **cuts** or **burns**, apply calendula gel directly to the wound to speed healing and soothe pain.

- For **skin problems** such as **eczema** or **psoriasis**, use a calendula-based cream twice a day to reduce inflammation and irritation.

- For **sore throats**, make calendula tea by infusing a tablespoon of dried flowers in a cup of hot water. Strain and drink up to three times a day.

- To relieve **menstrual pain,** drink calendula tea regularly.

- For **eye infections,** make an infusion with a handful of calendula flowers and use as an eye lotion.

- For **insect bites,** apply calendula ointment to reduce itching and swelling.

- To treat **acne** and **skin blemishes**, apply diluted calendula oil locally to the affected areas.

CALENDULA IN COOKING

Spring salad with calendula

INGREDIENTS: 150 g baby lettuce, a handful of calendula petals, 1 tbsp balsamic vinegar, 3 tbsp olive oil, 1 tsp honey, salt, pepper.

- Rinse and spin-dry the lettuce shoots.

- Scatter the calendula petals on top.

- In a bowl, combine the balsamic vinegar, olive oil, honey, salt and pepper to make a vinaigrette.

- Drizzle the vinaigrette over the salad just before serving.

- Enjoy this colorful, fragrant salad to brighten up your spring meals!

GARLIC
(ALLIUM SATIVUM)

THE WONDERS OF A CONDIMENT WITH A THOUSAND VIRTUES

Finally, let's discover garlic, a condiment famous not only for its unique taste and pungent aroma, but also for its countless medicinal virtues, known and respected for millennia.

Garlic originated in Central Asia and is one of the oldest medicinal remedies known to mankind. As far back as 3000 BC, the Sumerians recorded the therapeutic virtues of garlic on cuneiform tablets. As for the Egyptians, they gave it to the slaves building the pyramids to strengthen their constitution. Garlic was also considered a sacred medicinal plant by the Greeks and Romans, who used it to treat a multitude of illnesses. It gradually spread throughout the world over the ages, and each culture adapted and used it in its own way. Today, it is a key ingredient in cuisines the world over, adding not only flavor to dishes, but also significant medicinal value.

In the kitchen

Garlic is a staple of many of the world's cuisines, offering incomparable aroma and flavor. It is particularly appreciated in Mediterranean cuisine, where it is often used in sauces, stir-fries and stews. It is rich in **vitamins C and B6**, **manganese**, **selenium** and contains **sulfur compounds**, which are responsible for its **antimicrobial** and **anti-inflammatory properties**. Indeed, garlic is renowned for its ability to **fight infection**, boost **the immune system**, reduce **cholesterol**, and may even play a role in **preventing certain cancers**. It also has **antifungal properties** and is a **powerful antioxidant**, making it useful against cardiovascular disease. Garlic can be eaten raw, cooked, or in powder and oil form, and each form has its own specific benefits. But beware: in large quantities, garlic can irritate the digestive tract. What's more, its consumption can lead to specific breath and body odor, but its health benefits are such that it would be a shame to go without. To maximize its benefits, it's best eaten raw and crushed or cut, as this activates its beneficial compounds. However, cooking does not destroy all its active components, and has the advantage of making its taste milder and sweeter, making it suitable for a variety of dishes.

TREATING YOURSELF WITH GARLIC

- For **high blood pressure,** eat raw, minced or crushed garlic regularly, as it may help reduce blood pressure.

- For **colds,** eat a clove of raw garlic with honey twice a day until symptoms improve.

- For **fungal infections** such as athlete's foot, apply garlic gel or diluted garlic oil to the affected area.

- To reduce **cholesterol,** eat 2 to 3 cloves of raw garlic a day.

- For an **upset stomach,** take garlic with water or honey to soothe inflammation and fight bacteria.

- For **skin problems** such as acne, apply diluted garlic oil to pimples.

- For **warts,** place a slice of garlic on the wart, cover with a bandage and leave overnight.

GARLIC IN THE KITCHEN

Spaghetti with garlic and parsley

INGREDIENTS: 400 g spaghetti, 4 garlic cloves, 4 tbsp olive oil, 1 bunch fresh parsley, salt, pepper.

1. Cook spaghetti according to package instructions.

2. Meanwhile, peel and finely chop the garlic.

3. In a frying pan, sauté the chopped garlic in olive oil until golden.

4. Chop the parsley and add to the garlic, sautéing for 1-2 minutes.

5. Drain the pasta and toss with the garlic and parsley mixture.

6. Season with salt and pepper to taste, serve hot and enjoy!

CONCLUSION

Dear Readers,

As you close this book, I hope you will take away with you a deeper knowledge of, and greater respect for, the incredible world of medicinal plants. Plants are humanity's silent companions, ever present, generously offering their benefits, whether as food, medicine or inspiration.

Over the pages, we've traveled together through the vast lands of the plant kingdom, exploring medicinal spices, traditional Chinese herbs, and other popular medicinal plants. Each plant unveiled is a promise of discovery, healing and a rewarding relationship with the natural world.

It is our responsibility to protect and preserve this precious natural heritage, in order to pass on the wisdom of plants to future generations. By cultivating a conscious and respectful relationship with nature, we not only promote our individual well-being, but also contribute to the balance and harmony of our planet.

I hope you've found inspiration and enlightenment in these pages, and that you're now better equipped to explore the fascinating world of medicinal plants for yourself. May every grain of turmeric, every mint leaf, every lavender flower remind you of the richness and diversity of the plant world.

Perhaps you now feel the call of plants, inviting you to deepen your knowledge, experiment and create. I encourage you to answer this call, to immerse yourself in the study and practice of herbalism, and to share your discoveries and experiences with those around you.

Remember, plants are our allies, guiding and supporting us on our path to optimal health and inner balance. By honoring medicinal plants, we honor life itself, in all its diversity and complexity.

It's time, dear readers, to reap the rewards of your new knowledge, to put the teachings of this book into practice, and to take part in the ancestral exchange between man and plant. May your journey into the world of medicinal plants be a lifelong adventure of learning, healing and discovery.

I leave you with the hope that you will continue to explore, learn and grow with plants. May these pages be the beginning of an enriching dialogue and a lasting partnership with the plant world. And remember, nature is an open book, waiting to be read, on every street corner, in every garden, in every forest.

Be curious, be respectful, and above all, be amazed.

With all my gratitude and best wishes for your botanical journey,

Sébastien Mallet.

Thanks

I would like to express my gratitude to all those who have made this book possible. To the many researchers and authors who have preserved and interpreted this art of consuming medicinal plants. To the publishing team who carefully crafted every page of this book. And above all, to you, dear readers, for your interest.

Give your honest opinion on Amazon!

Your suggestions and criticisms are invaluable.

They make every reading experience even more satisfying!

Thank you very much for reading my book.

I wish you all the success you deserve!

Source Images

The author and publisher would particularly like to thank the following websites:

www.pxhere.com/

www.freepik.com

Printed in Great Britain
by Amazon